PagePlus 11 User Guide

How to Contact Us

Our main office (UK, Europe):

The Software Centre
PO Box 2000, Nottingham, NG11 7GW, UK

Main	(0115) 914 2000
Registration (UK only)	(0800) 376 1989
Sales (UK only)	(0800) 376 7070
Technical Support (UK only)	(0845) 345 6770
Customer Service (UK only)	(0845) 345 6770
Customer Service/ Technical Support (International)	+44 115 914 9090
General Fax	(0115) 914 2020
Technical Support e-mail	support@serif.co.uk

American office (USA, Canada):

The Software Center
13 Columbia Drive, Suite 5, Amherst, NH 03031

Main	(603) 889-8650
Registration	(800) 794-6876
Sales	(800) 55-SERIF or 557-3743
Technical Support	(603) 886-6642
Customer Service	(800) 489-6720
General Fax	(603) 889-1127
Technical Support e-mail	support@serif.com

Online

Visit us on the Web at	http://www.serif.com
Serif newsgroups	news://news.serif.com

International

Please contact your local distributor/dealer. For further details please contact us at one of our phone numbers above.

Comments or other feedback

We want to hear from you! Please e-mail **feedback@serif.com** with your ideas and comments!

This document, and the software described in it, is furnished under an end user License Agreement, which is included with the product. The agreement specifies the permitted and prohibited uses.

© 2005 Serif (Europe) Ltd. All rights reserved. No part of this publication may be reproduced in any form without the express written permission of Serif (Europe) Ltd.

All Serif product names are trademarks of Serif (Europe) Ltd. Microsoft, Windows and the Windows logo are registered trademarks of Microsoft Corporation. All other trademarks acknowledged.

Serif PagePlus 11.0 © 2005 Serif (Europe) Ltd.

Companies and names used in samples are fictitious.

Clipart samples from Serif ArtPacks © Serif (Europe) Ltd. & Paul Harris

Portions images © 1997-2002 Nova Development Corporation; © 1995 Expressions Computer Software; © 1996-98 CreatiCom, In.; 1996 Cliptoart; © 1996-99 Hemera; © 1997 Multimedia Agency Corporation; © 1997-98 Seattle Support Group. Rights of all parties reserved.

Digital image content© 2005 JupiterImages Corporation. All Rights Reserved.

Portions TrueType Font content © 2002 Arts & Letters Corporation. All Rights Reserved.

Bitstream Font content © 1981-2005 Bitstream Inc. All rights reserved.

Panose Typeface Matching System ©1991, 1992, 1995-97 Hewlett-Packard Corporation.

Portions graphics import/export technology © AccuSoft Corp. & Eastman Kodak Company & LEAD Technologies, Inc.

THE PROXIMITY HYPHENATION SYSTEM © 1989 Proximity Technology Inc. All rights reserved.

THE PROXIMITY/COLLINS DATABASE® © 1990 William Collins Sons & Co. Ltd.; © 1990 Proximity Technology Inc. All rights reserved.

THE PROXIMITY/MERRIAM-WEBSTER DATABASE® © 1990 Merriam-Webster Inc.; © 1990 Proximity Technology Inc. All rights reserved.

The Sentry Spelling-Checker Engine © 2000 Wintertree Software Inc.

The ThesDB Thesaurus Engine © 1993-97 Wintertree Software Inc.

WGrammar Grammar-Checker Engine © 1998 Wintertree Software Inc.

PANTONE® Colours displayed in the software application or in the user documentation may not match PANTONE-identified standards. Consult current PANTONE Colour Publications for accurate colour. PANTONE® and other Pantone, Inc. trademarks are the property of Pantone, Inc. © Pantone Inc., 2001.

Pantone, Inc. is the copyright owner of colour data and/or software which are licensed to Serif (Europe) Ltd. to distribute for use only in combination with PagePlus. PANTONE Colour Data and/or Software shall not be copied onto another disk or into memory unless as part of the execution of PagePlus.

Contents

1. Welcome 1
About the User Guide 3
What's New in PagePlus 11.0.. 4
Established features 6
Registration, Upgrades, and Support 11
Installation 11

2. Getting Started 13
Startup Wizard 15
Creating a publication from Design Templates......................... 16
Starting a new publication from scratch................................... 16
Opening an existing publication 17
Working with more than one publication 17
Saving your publication 18
Using PagePlus templates.. 18
Closing PagePlus.. 19
Customising the Workspace 19

3. Working with Pages 23
Setting up a publication.. 25
Understanding master pages.. 26
Viewing pages... 28
Navigating 30
Adding, removing, and rearranging pages................................ 31
Working with layers... 32
Setting guides for page margins, rows, columns, and bleeds ... 39
Using the rulers and dot grid.. 41
Snapping... 44
Using headers and footers 44
Using page numbering.. 45
Updating and saving defaults 46
Setting PagePlus options.. 47

4. Working with Objects 49
What are Objects?.. 51
Selecting an object... 51
Selecting multiple objects 52
Creating groups 53

Contents

Copying, pasting, and duplicating objects 53
Moving objects 55
Resizing objects 57
Locking an object's size or position 59
Arranging Objects 59
Aligning and distributing objects 60
Converting an object to a picture 61
Exporting as a picture 62
Rotating an object 63
Flipping an object 64
Cropping and combining objects 64
Applying a mesh warp envelope 67

5. Working with Text   69

Importing text from a file 71
Understanding text frames 72
Using artistic text 78
Putting text on a path 79
Editing text on the page 83
Editing story text with WritePlus 86
Using Find and Replace 87
Inserting footnotes and endnotes 88
Formatting 88
Using text styles 89
Adjusting letter spacing and kerning 92
Fitting text to frames 93
Wrapping text to an object 94
Creating a bulleted or numbered list 96
Creating ruled lines 97
Using AutoCorrect and AutoSpell 101
Spell-checking 103
Automatic proofreading 105
Using the thesaurus 105
Previewing the printed page 106
Working with Tables 107
Creating a table of contents 116
Creating an index 117
Producing a book with BookPlus 118
Using mail merge 123
Checking fonts and resources used 124

6. Working with Images, Lines and Shapes   129

Importing images 131
Applying adjustments.. 133
Using the Gallery 136
Drawing and editing lines.. 139
Setting line properties 143
Drawing and editing shapes.. 145
Applying shadows, glow, bevel/emboss, colour fill 148
Using 3D filter effects.. 149
Understanding blend modes 152
Feathering... 155
Adding dimensionality (Instant 3D) 156
Adding borders.. 157
Using object styles 158

7. Using Colours and Fills   161

Applying solid colours 163
Working with gradient and Bitmap fills.................................... 164
Using colour schemes... 169
Managing publication colours and palettes............................. 172
Working with transparency.. 175
Colour Matching with Pantone or Serif Colours...................... 179
Managing Screen and Output Colours 180

8. Printing your Publication   183

Printing basics... 185
Previewing the printed page 186
Printing special formats... 187
Generating professional output... 189
Saving print profiles 190

9. Using PDF   191

Exporting PDF files 193
Importing PDF files 193
Creating a PDF bookmark list 195
Using PDF Forms 196

Contents

10. Producing Web Pages   217

Getting started in Web mode 219
Hyperlinking an object 220
Viewing hyperlinks in your publication 221
Adding hotspots 221
Adding rollovers 222
Rollover options 223
Choosing Web site colours 224
Setting Web picture display options 225
Choosing page properties 226
Adding animation effects 226
Adding sound and video 227
Adding Java applets 227
Adding HTML 229
Adding search engine descriptors 229
Publishing a Web site to a local folder 230
Previewing your Web site in a browser 230
Publishing to the World Wide Web 231
Maintaining your Web site 233

Index   235

Welcome

1

Welcome to PagePlus 11—still the best value in a complete desktop publishing package for your home, school, church, or growing business. PagePlus 11 "does it all" more easily than ever! If you're just starting out as a desktop publisher, we've got automated Wizards for just about every job. If you require professional-level features and total control, we can offer those as well!

From glossy corporate marketing materials and elegant Web sites to fun stuff like party invitations, PagePlus 11 can handle it... Ads, brochures, business stationery, cards, letterheads, compliment slips, invoices, flyers, forms, newsletters, notices, handouts, posters, banners, price lists, reports, announcements, invitations, greeting cards—even Web sites and so much more. With just your PC, printer, and PagePlus, you can save time and money.

About the User Guide

This *User Guide* is your guide to getting started and getting results with PagePlus 11—from the basics to advanced professional printing.

- 1. **Welcome to PagePlus!** Introduces you to general program information and key PagePlus features in this release.

- 2. **Getting Started**. The basics to get you up and running in no time— including create, open, save, and close your publication.

- 3. **Working with Pages**. Create and manage pages/master pages, layers, headers/footers and page numbering.

- 4. **Working with Objects**. Manipulate objects on the page.

- 5. **Working with Text**. Learn how to apply text to the page, including how to use supporting tools for text management (i.e., spelling, auto correct, amongst many others)

- 6. **Working with Images, Lines and Shapes**. Drawing and editing is covered, as is image adjustments, 3D effects, and use of styles.

- 7. **Using Colours and Fills**. Apply colour to an object's fill, line and text.

- 8. **Printing your Publication**. How to get the best results using desktop printing or professional output, colour options, and more.

- 9. **Using PDF**. Find out how to import and export PDF documents, as well as use PDF technology for state-of-the-art dynamic form handling.

- 10. **Producing Web Pages**. Beyond the basics—tips and techniques for optimising your Web site's design and impact.

What's New in PagePlus 11.0

- **Import and Edit PDF Files easily** (p. 193)
  Use PagePlus's ground breaking and extremely powerful **PDF import** feature to open PDF documents as new PagePlus publications or insert a PDF document's contents into existing publications. Either way, PDF contents can be easily edited within PagePlus—the text and paragraph formatting of the original PDF document is maintained.

- **Automatic Font Substitution** (p. 125)
  PANOSE©-matching substitution of fonts on import resolves possible missing font issues with the option of manually re-mapping fonts with the Resource Manager at a later date. **Serif Font Map** files, which store your preferred font substitutions, can be exported for use in other PagePlus publications. Equally, importing of existing map files is a great time-saving feature.

- **PDF Forms for electronic form completion** (p. 196)
  Create and **publish PDF forms** from within PagePlus— membership forms, invoices, surveys, and many other form types can all be enhanced with added text fields, buttons, check boxes, lists, and radio buttons designed for electronic submission. Form recipients can fill-out a circulated electronic form and print, save and/or submit their form data across the Web or to your e-mail address using "**Serif Web Resources**", which provides web-to-email service for registered Serif customers. Creating submittable forms is a snap using PagePlus's easy to follow **Form Submit Wizard**. For document security, the generated forms can be certified (by accredited bodies or self-certified) by author and signed by form recipients.

- **Image adjustments** (p. 133)
  Benefit from "on-board" image adjustments for **quick colour correction** of imported images and objects converted to pictures—pick from Auto Levels, Auto Contrast, Brightness/Contrast, Channel Mixer, Colour Balance, Curves, and many more. Commonly used **special effects** such as Diffuse Glow, Dust and Scratch Remover, Shadows/Highlights, and various blurs make up the set of adjustments, which can be applied in combination. You can now eliminate the dreaded red eye effect on subjects in your photos with the new **Red Eye Tool** with a single click. If you want to do even more, use the handy **Edit in PhotoPlus** option from within PagePlus to edit and save images and PhotoPlus files with impressive synergy.

- **Table Enhancements** (from p. 107)
  Display data from databases directly with the new **Database Import Wizard**. Rotate text within cells, improved copying and pasting between cells (includes direct pasting of Microsoft Excel spreadsheet cells into PagePlus and HTML tables as well). Drag and drop support between cells lets you replicate text to other cells—for more power, use drag and Shift to replicate all text and cell formatting to other cells simultaneously.

- **Multilingual Support** (p. 103)
  PagePlus can now cope with multiple language documents (over 10 dictionaries are provided including German, French, Spanish, and Italian). You can mark words, paragraphs or whole stories with a language and PagePlus will automatically check the spelling for you in that language. Mix and match multiple languages in one document if you want.

- **Design Templates** (p. 16)
  Turn your photo collection into beautiful printed documents using the new range of **Photo Scrapbook pages** provided. Existing templates have been redesigned with eye-catching new fonts. Sixty-three new high quality fonts are now included with PagePlus. View the wizard collection in detail with the new zooming design template browser.

- **New User Interface**
  PagePlus has undergone major rework to ensure all the information you need for efficient use is at your fingertips. A whole series of **dockable Studio tabs** now replace the Studio toolbar and ChangeBar hosted in previous PagePlus versions. These provide single-click access to commonly used settings such as Line, Opacity, and Colour. The Pages tab has been revitalized with an optional preview/layout mode. Layer management is now carried out exclusively via the **Layers tab**. Use the Gallery to store your favourite designs for use in any publication! Alignment controls are now conveniently placed on the new **Align tab**.

- Every tab can be docked/undocked, groups with other tabs, resized in any direction or shown/hidden. You can also create different configurations of these tabs and save them as **separate workspaces** for instant recall whenever you wish.

- **Context Bar** (p. 22)
  PagePlus now supports context bars whose tools and options dynamically change according to the currently selected object in your publication. This ensures that the most common options are always at your fingertips.

- **Colour Swatches** (p. 161)
  PagePlus now provides **10 extra coordinated themed palettes** which can be seen in the **Swatches tab**—you can even add, view, edit or delete colours you have been using in your publication from within the Publication palette!

- **..and some very useful improvements you've been asking for!!**
  Opening a Publication via the Startup Wizard sports a new dialog, providing Folder and History views; Thumbnail views are supported equally. **Import Photoshop .PSD files** with clipped paths into PagePlus. You can also now open and manipulate **CMYK .JPG** files without conversion to RGB.

Established features

DTP revolutionised the graphics arts industry, and PagePlus revolutionised the DTP market—with high-impact design available to everyone. Features such as...

- **Books Have Arrived on Your Desktop!**
  Treat separate PagePlus publication files as chapters and use the **BookPlus** utility to link them into a book!

- **Mail Merge**
  With Mail and Photo Merge, read data from just about any source: tables from HTML Web pages, database files, even live ODBC servers!

- **Use Layers to Make the Most of Your Content**
  Each page can have **multiple layers**—so you can assign elements to different layers for modular design.

- **Superior Text Entry and Unicode Support**
  Import, paste, export in **Unicode** format... design with foreign-language or special fonts and characters.

- **Augmented Text Editing Capabilities, Convenience**
  Instantly fill new frames with "dummy" text for pre-final layout design, or click the **AutoFlow** button anytime to generate new frames and pages for longer stories. Use drag-and-drop editing in WritePlus. Clear formatting (revert to plain style) with a single keystroke. Enhanced **Find and Replace** features "wild card" capability using regular expressions.

- **Improved Clipboard and Object Controls**
  The **Paste in Place** command lets you manipulate objects more efficiently. Between objects, align and snap to object centres... use **Paste Format** to transfer any or all attributes. On single objects, apply a **border** to selected edges... include or exclude specific filter effects.

- **Picture Import and Editing Enhancements**
  Import images at 96dpi screen resolution. Adjust brightness and contrast, size and resolution, apply colouration or transparency, view properties with the **Picture context bar**. Copy/paste inline images in text, adjust alignment and text wrap.

- **Versatile Setup with Auto-Imposition**
  Just click to specify layouts for small (business cards and labels), folded (booklets and greetings cards), and large publications (banners and posters). You see your publications the right way up on-screen—and let PagePlus take care of **orienting and ordering the printed output** for correctly assembled masters!

- **Intelligent Colour Schemes**
  Choose from dozens of preset **colour schemes** to change the overall appearance of your publications with a single click. You can customise the scheme colours, create brand new schemes, and apply any scheme to a "from-scratch" publication.

- **Object Styles Transform with a Single Click**
  Select any object (including text) and choose from a gallery of ready-made styles that **combine a host of attributes** such as 3D filter effects, glows, shadows, textures, and materials. Customise the preset styles or create your own!

- **Web Publishing Mode**
  Create your own Web site using web-based Design Templates or convert an existing PagePlus publication to a Web site! The Layout Checker helps you fine-tune your design. Preview your site in a Web browser and publish it to a local folder or a remote server. Use FTP-based **maintenance mode** with familiar Explorer-style controls.

- **PDF Output for Pro Printing or Electronic Distribution...**
  Press-ready PDF/X file includes all fonts and colour information for spot or process colour... and PDF ensures a secure, cross-platform electronic alternative to paper-based publishing, with Bookmarks, PageHints, and file protection! Add Web-style **hyperlinks** directly... automatically generate a **bookmark list** (table of contents) using styled text markup. Export with optional PDF streaming for faster Web-based downloads!

- **Frame Text and Artistic Text**
  Compose traditional **text in frames**, rotate or reshape frames and still edit their text. And **artistic text** lets you click and type anywhere on the page, format with the customary tools, then apply colourful lines and fills directly at the character level. Scale it, rotate it, flip it... **flow it along a path**!

- **Text Composition Tools**
  PagePlus includes word count, search and replace, spell-checking, thesaurus, and proof reader.

- **Professional Layout Tools**
  Multipage view lets you **see an array of pages**, not just one at a time. Intelligent text fitting. Movable rulers and guides. Precision placement, rotation, and **text wrap**. Flip, crop, watermark, and recolour graphics. Text formatting with bullets, lists, kerning, hyphenation, drop caps, smart quotes, and named styles. Multiple master pages with **as many separate background templates as you need**. Facing pages display, and much more!

- **QuickShapes**
  As with other Serif solutions, **QuickShapes** provide intelligent clipart for your publication.

- **Powerful Drawing Options**
  Sketch **freehand lines and curves**, extend existing lines with ease... simply "connect the dots" to **trace around curved objects** and pictures. Use the Curve context bar to **fine-tune contours or edit Bézier nodes**. Sketch using **calligraphic lines**, add rounded corners (caps), vary the join style of connected lines. Connect end points to create any shape you like! Apply **line styles** to all kinds of shapes—even add line endings like arrowheads and diamonds. Customise line and fill, apply transparency, even freely edit the outline. Automatic anti-aliasing of lines, text, and polygons results in superb visuals, both on-screen and on the printed page.

- **Powerful Shape Conversion Options**
  The **Convert to Curves** command gives you node-and-segment control over all objects, including QuickShapes. **Convert to Shaped Frame** lets you create a text container out of any shape you can draw! And with **Crop to Shape** you can use any top shape's outline to trim another below. And try **combining curves** to create "holes" for mask or stencil effects.

- **A New Slant with Enveloping**
  Apply a customisable **mesh warp envelope** to any object to add perspective, slant, bulge, and more.

- **Gradient and Bitmap Fills**
  For sophisticated illustrations and impressive typographic effects, select from a wide variety of **Linear, Radial, Conical,** and **Bitmap fills**.

- **Transparency Effects**
  Both **solid and variable transparency** let you add new depth to your print and Web creations. Apply transparency directly from the Opacity tab, then edit nodes and opacity with the interactive tool. Get set for fun with Photo Edge Effects and a host of other Bitmap transparencies!

- **Astounding 3D Lighting and Surface Effects**
  Beyond **shadow, glow, bevel, and emboss**, advanced algorithms **bring flat shapes to life**! Choose one or more effects, then vary surface and source light properties. Start with a pattern or a function, adjust parameters for incredible surface contours, textures, fills— realistic-looking wood, water, skin, marble and much more. The **Feathering** filter effect adds a soft or blurry edge to any object. **Instant 3D** adds realistic depth to ordinary objects and text. Use one master control panel to vary extrusion, rotation, bevel, lighting, texture, and more.

- **Versatile Text Shape and Flow**
  You can **rotate or reshape text frames** and still edit their text. Enhanced **text wrap options** and separate crop and wrap outlines mean you have greater control over where text flows and how it appears.

- **Impressive Graphics Handling**
  Import images inline as part of frame text flow, and create your own 32-bit anti-aliased TIFFs and PNGs. **Convert to Picture** allows instant, in-place format changes! Control imported metafiles and OLE options. TIFFs retain CMYK colour data for full colour separation. Linked images are easy to maintain... and each export filter remembers its own settings. For more accurate results with professional printing, you can **switch in a flash** to a CMYK palette... add your own colours and save custom palettes for global use... load saved palettes right from the Tools menu.

- **Photo Optimiser**
  If your publication includes colour or greyscale photographs, use the Photo Optimiser to get the best results for each photo on your particular printer. Pick the best result from the thumbnail sheet—and PagePlus remembers the optimum settings for that image!

- **Table Tool with Editable Calendars**
  Create and edit tables, with no need for a separate utility. Choose from a range of preset formats or design your own by customising lines, cells, rows, and columns. Use the convenient Table Toolbar to enter text, apply **preset or custom number formatting**, and choose from **functions** for spreadsheet calculations. Powerful text manipulation features... and calendars are table-based for enhanced functionality!

- **Index, Table of Contents, Border and Calendar Wizards**
  Compile a professional **index** complete with headings, subheadings, and page references... especially useful for longer publications! Automatically collect newsletter headlines (or any styled text you specify) into a **table of contents** list! **Add instant borders** to your imported pictures and shape art. Choose from a wide variety of sizes and design options, then just click and drag to fit your **calendar** to a column or a whole page!

- **Versatile Desktop Printing and Mail Merge**
  Impressive results on your dot-matrix, ink-jet, or laser printer in black and white or full colour. Print your current publication multiple times, **merging data** from any character-delimited address list file.

- **Total Ease-of-Use**
  PagePlus features MDI (Multiple Document Interface). Mouse wheel support. Hideable, customisable toolbars for extra workspace area. Right-click menus. AutoCorrect and AutoSpell proofing options. And there's more: The **Replicate tool** instantly multiplies any object into a line or grid arrangement. You can drag and drop objects from other applications, select multiple Undo and Redo actions selectable from a handy list.

Registration, Upgrades, and Support

If you see the Registration Wizard when you launch PagePlus, please take a moment to complete the registration process. Just call Serif free phone and provide the installation number and code shown. We'll give you a personalised registration number in return. Remember, if you need technical support please contact us. We aim to provide fast, friendly service and knowledgeable help.

Installation

System Requirements

If you need help installing Windows, or setting up peripherals, see Windows documentation and help.

Minimum:

- IBM-compatible Pentium PC with CD-ROM drive and mouse (or other Microsoft-compatible pointing device)
- Microsoft Windows® 98 SE, Me, 2000, or XP operating system
- 64MB RAM minimum
- 240MB (recommended install) free hard disk space
- SVGA (800x600 resolution, 16-bit colour) display or higher.

Additional disk resources and memory are required when editing large or complex documents.

Optional:

- Windows-compatible printer
- TWAIN-compatible scanner and/or digital camera
- Stylus or other input device
- Internet account and connection required for Web Publishing features and accessing online resources

First-time Install

To install PagePlus 11, simply insert the Program CD-ROM into your CD-ROM drive. The AutoRun feature automatically starts the Setup process and all you need to do is answer the on-screen questions. If the AutoRun does not start the install, use the manual install instructions below.

If you've also obtained the *PagePlus 11 Resource CD* (see below), install it now following the same procedure you used for the Program CD.

Manual Install/Re-install

To re-install the software or to change any part of the installation at a later date, select **Control Panel** from the Windows **Start** menu (via the **Settings** item for pre-XP systems) and then double-click the **Add/Remove Programs** icon. Make sure the correct CD-ROM is inserted into your CD-ROM drive, choose **Serif PagePlus 11**, and click the **Install...** button. You'll have the choice of removing or adding components, re-installing components, or removing all components.

Other PagePlus Resources

Resource CD-ROM

The *Resource CD* includes hundreds of professionally designed Wizard documents for instantly creating brochures, business forms, calendars, stationery, notices, newsletters, Web sites, and much more. In addition, you'll find a set of illustrated tutorials for a hands-on introduction to the full range of PagePlus features.

Resource Guide

The *Resource Guide* provides a compendium of reference material to help any user get the most out of PagePlus. At-a-glance, full colour previews of PagePlus Wizards, Schemes, Object Styles and more... convenient access to a range of tutorials at all levels... the Guide is something to keep handy and return to time and time again.

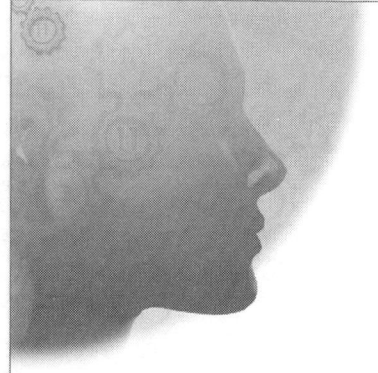

Getting Started

2

Once PagePlus has been installed, you'll be ready to start. Setup adds a **Serif PagePlus 11** item to the **(All) Programs** submenu of the Windows **Start** menu.

- Use the Windows **Start** button to start PagePlus (or if PagePlus is already running, choose **New>New from Startup Wizard...** from the File menu) to display the Startup Wizard (menu screen).

Startup Wizard

The Startup Wizard presents five choices:

- **use a design template**, to create an instant document from a design
- **start from scratch**, to get a blank page to work on
- **open a publication**, to edit your saved PagePlus files
- **view tutorials**, to see introductory illustrated overviews
- **visit web site**, to link to support and product information

To get started, click on **start from scratch**.

Creating a publication from Design Templates

It's so much easier creating publications with a little bit of help—PagePlus comes complete with a whole range of categorised design templates which will speed you through the creation of all kinds of publications for desktop or professional printing—even your own Web site! PagePlus ships with a selection of Design Templates, and many more are available on the *PagePlus 11 Resource CD*.

To create a publication from a design template:

1. Launch PagePlus, or choose **New...** from the File menu and select **New from Startup Wizard...**.

2. Click **use a design template**.

3. Select a publication category on the left, and examine the samples on the right. Click the sample that's closest to what you want, then click **Finish**.

> NOTE: The above method is the only way to access Design Templates. If you've switched the Startup Wizard off (and don't see it when you start up or choose **File/New...**), you can switch it on again. Choose **Options...** from the Tools menu and check **use startup wizard** on the General tab.

Starting a new publication from scratch

Although **Design Templates** can simplify your design choices, you can just as easily start out from scratch with a new, blank publication.

To start a new publication of a certain type:

1. Launch PagePlus, or choose **New...** from the File menu and select **New from Startup Wizard.....**

2. Click **start from scratch**.

3. Select a publication type on the left and examine the samples on the right. Click the one that's closest to what you want, you can select from the given publication types or define a custom publication by clicking Custom Page Setup.

4. Click **Finish** to open the new publication with a blank page.

> TIP: If you click Cancel (or press Escape) from the Startup Wizard, you'll get a blank document using default page properties.

To start a new default publication:

- Click the 📄 **New Publication** button on the Standard toolbar.

To turn off the Startup Wizard:

- Choose **Options** from the Tools menu and uncheck **Use Startup Wizard** on the General page.

Opening an existing publication

You can open an existing PagePlus publication either from the Startup Wizard or from within PagePlus.

To open an existing publication from the Startup Wizard:

1. Select the **open a publication** option. In the Documents pane of the **Open Saved Work** dialog, you'll see either your computer's folder structure for navigation to your publications (Folders tab) or a list of most recently used PagePlus publications (History tab). Preview thumbnails can be shown in the adjacent pane.

2. Click a file name or sample, then click **Finish**.
   OR
   Click **Browse** to locate a different file. In the Open dialog, select the folder and file name and click the **Open** button.

To open an existing publication from within PagePlus:

1. Click the 📂 **Open** button on the Standard toolbar.

2. In the Open dialog, select the folder and file name and click the **Open** button.

To revert to the saved version of an open publication:

- Choose **Revert...** from the File menu.

Working with more than one publication

PagePlus lets you open more than one publication at a time, and work with more than one window for a given publication. You can drag and drop objects between publication windows.

Each new publication you open appears in a separate window with its own settings.

To close the current window:

- Choose **Close** from the File menu or click the window's **Close** button. If it's the only window open for the publication, the command closes the publication and you'll be prompted to save changes.

> NOTE: You can close all open publications without exiting the main PagePlus application.

The **Window** menu lets you create new windows and arrange the open document windows, i.e. by cascading or tiling horizontally or vertically.

Saving your publication

To save your work:

- Click the **Save** button on the Standard toolbar.
  OR
  To save under a different name, choose **Save As...** from the File menu.

Using PagePlus templates

Once you've settled on a particular layout, you can save the layout as a PagePlus **template** to be used as a basis for other publications. You can save any PagePlus publication as a PagePlus template (*.PPX) file. When opening a saved template file, PagePlus automatically opens an untitled copy, leaving the original template intact.

Templates help ensure continuity between publications by preserving starting setups for such elements as page layout, contents, styles, and colour palettes.

To save a publication as a template:

- Choose **Save As...** from the File menu. Under "Save as type:" click to select the **PagePlus Template (*.ppx)** option. Enter a file name, leaving the .PPX extension intact, and click **Save**.

> TIP: If you want a custom PPX template to appear as a publication type when you choose **start from scratch** from the Startup Wizard, save it in the "\PageTypes\My Templates" subfolder of your "PagePlus\11.0\" installation.

To open a template file:

1. Choose **Open...** from the File menu and select **PagePlus Templates (*.ppx)** in the "Files of type" box.
2. If you want to open the original template (wizard) file, uncheck the **Open as Untitled** option. To open an untitled copy, leave the box checked.
3. Click the **Open** button.

Closing PagePlus

To close the current window:

- Choose **Close** from the File menu or click the window's 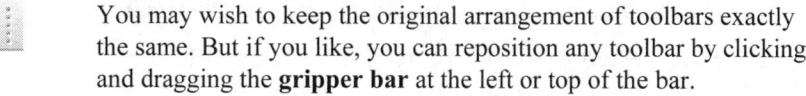 **Close** button. If it's the only window open for the publication, the command closes the publication and you'll be prompted to save changes.

To close PagePlus:

- Choose **Exit** from the File menu.

You'll be prompted to save changes to any open publications.

Customising the Workspace

PagePlus is supplied with a default arrangement of PagePlus toolbars and Studio tabs, which are initially arranged in a convenient layout around the perimeter of the work area. However, you have full control over this arrangement, and can customise the display any way you want—by showing or hiding toolbars and tabs, or repositioning them onscreen in a way that suits your style.

Customising toolbars

To show (or hide) a toolbar:

1. Choose **Toolbars** from the View menu.
2. Check (or uncheck) the toolbar name.

   You may wish to keep the original arrangement of toolbars exactly the same. But if you like, you can reposition any toolbar by clicking and dragging the **gripper bar** at the left or top of the bar.

Toolbars can float anywhere onscreen, or dock (join) with the edges of the PagePlus window.

To dock a toolbar:
1. Click its gripper bar and drag to the desired location.
2. Drop the item into position when the interface responds.

The Options dialog includes command icons and other items you can assign to any toolbar. Note that certain toolbars (MailMerge) and context bars (e.g., Curve, Picture, Frame, etc.) are only displayed under program control in specific modes.

To add an item to a toolbar:
1. Choose **Options...** from the Tools menu, expand the **Toolbars** category, and select the **Customise** page.
2. Select a category to view the items available for that category.
3. Click any command icon or item to see its description.
4. To add an item to a toolbar, drag it directly onto the toolbar. An "I-beam" mark appears to guide you in placing the item precisely.

To remove an item from a toolbar:
- Simply drag it off the toolbar (there's no need to open the Options dialog).

To create a new toolbar:
1. Choose **Options...** from the Tools menu and select the **Toolbars** page.
2. Click **New....**
3. Type a name for the new toolbar and click **OK**.

OR

- Follow the steps above for adding an item to a toolbar, but instead of dragging an item to a toolbar, drag it to a non-toolbar region. The item becomes the first one on a new toolbar with a default name.

To remove a custom toolbar:
1. Choose **Options...** from the Tools menu and select the **Toolbars** page.
2. Select the custom toolbar to be removed and click **Delete**.

To reset all toolbars to their default arrangements:
1. Choose **Options...** from the Tools menu and select the **Toolbars** page.
2. Click **Reset**.

Customising Studio tabs

Initially, the tabs appear as a group at the right edge of the workspace. In this form the three groupings behave as single multi-tabbed toolbars, including a **gripper bar** (see above) next to the left-most tab in the group. This lets you reposition the whole group.

You can undock individual tabs as floating "tab windows", group them into different group arrangements, and float/dock as toolbars anywhere on the workspace. Any tab or tab group can be collapsed or expanded by priority.

Within a given group of tabs, you can only view one tab's contents at a time. You can pick the arrangement that works best for you—separate tabs that you can view simultaneously, or grouped tabs to conserve screen space.

The **Auto Resizing Tabs** option in **Tools>Options** can be used to dynamically resize all tabs to the dimensions of a previously resized tab within the same tab group. Switch off the option to minimise the tab sizes within the same tab group.

To collapse/expand tabs:

1. Click the ▷ **Options** button on the right-hand corner of an individual tab's window or the entire tab group.

2. Select **Collapse** or **Expand** from the drop-down menu.

OR

- Click the tab name of a selected tab (either separate or in a group).

> TIP: **Tools>Options>Studio** lets you set the priority for the order in which tab's collapse.

To switch off specific tabs/all tabs in a group:

1. Click the ▷ **Options** button on the right-hand corner of the tab or tab group.

2. Select **Close** or **Close All** for a specific tab or tab group, respectively, from the drop-down menu.

To switch on/off all tabs completely:

1. Click the **Show/Hide Studio tabs** button on the bottom right-hand corner of the Hintline toolbar.

To dock/undock a tab:

- Double-click on the tab's label.

To reposition a floating tab on the screen:

- Drag the tab by its title bar to its new position.

To close a floating tab window:

- Click the window frame's ⊠ **Close** button.

Managing your Workspace

At some point in your session you may want to save the layout of your tabs in the current workspace, with respect to positioning, their size, whether they are switched on/off and if docked or not. This is easy to achieve by selecting **Studio Tabs>Save Workspace** in the View menu. The settings are saved to a Workspace file (*.wtb) to a folder of your choice.

At any point you can reset the workspace to its default state by selecting **Dock Tabs>Default Workspace** or load another previously saved Workspace .wtb file using **Studio Tabs>Load Workspace**; both options are available via the View menu.

Note that your PagePlus tool properties and view settings remain unaffected.

Using the Context Bar

The Context Bar brings commonly used options to hand. If you're performing an operation on a particular type of object, e.g. a picture, text, frame, curve, etc., its really time-saving and less cumbersome to use the Context Bar as a shortcut instead of navigating through menus. The Context Bar does this well and, as its name suggests, the options or tools shown will be specific to the currently selected object. As an example, the image adjustment or picture resize options are hosted on a Picture context bar for any selected image, i.e.

Simply deselect the image and the Context Bar will change to the Page context bar by default, or if a different object is selected, to the Context Bar for that object.

A whole variety of context bars may be displayed, i.e. Page, Picture, Text, Page, Frame, Curve, all provided to support the currently selected object.

As for other Toolbars, the context bar can be disabled if necessary (see **Customising toolbars** on p. 19).

Working with Pages

3

Setting up a publication

A publication's **page size** and **orientation** settings are fundamental to your layout, and are defined when the new publication is first created, either **using a design template** or as a **New Publication** choice via **File>New...** and the Startup Wizard. If the Startup Wizard is turned off, or you cancel the setup dialog, a new publication defaults to A4 (Europe) or Letter size (US). PagePlus can handle nearly unlimited page sizes. In practice, your working limit is likely to be set by the capabilities of your desktop printer.

To adjust size/orientation of the current publication (Paper Publishing mode):

1. Choose **Page Setup...** from the File menu.

2. For Regular publications, you can select a pre-defined paper size or enter custom values for page width and height, as well as setting the orientation (Portrait or Landscape).

3. For other publication types, you can select the publication types: Small (for example, business cards, labels, etc.), Large (banners or posters), or Folded (booklets).

4. Choose a pre-defined option from the list (use the preview) or to define a custom publication based on the selected option, click **Create Custom....**

5. Add additional custom settings if necessary.

6. Click **OK** to accept the new dimensions. The updated settings will be applied to the current publication.

To adjust size/orientation of the current publication (Web Publishing mode):

1. Choose **Page Setup...** from the File menu.

2. Set page dimensions as **Standard** for VGA monitors (recommended), **Wide** for SVGA, or **Custom**. For a custom setting, enter page dimensions in pixels.

Facing pages

In Paper Publishing mode, you can choose whether to set up your publication, such as books or booklets, so that the PagePlus window displays pages either singly or in pairs—as two facing pages side by side. You'll need facing pages if you're creating a publication where you need to see both the left-hand (verso) and right-hand (recto) pages, or one that employs double-page spreads where a headline or other element needs to run from the left-hand page to the right-hand page.

To set up facing pages (Paper Publishing mode):

- In the Page Setup dialog, check **Facing Pages**.

- If you plan to use background elements that span a double-page spread, check **Dual master pages**. This will let you define master pages with paired "left page" and "right page" components.
  OR
  For a facing-page layout where both left and right pages initially share the same master page, and you don't need to run background elements across the spread, uncheck **Dual master pages**.

Because you assign master pages to individual page layers, one page at a time, it takes two separate steps to assign a dual master page to both left and right facing pages. For details, see **Layers and master pages** on p. 35.

You can assign different master pages to the left and right publication pages if necessary. For example (see below), a left-hand "body text" page might use the left-side component of one master page, while a right-hand "chapter divider" page could use the right side of a different master page.

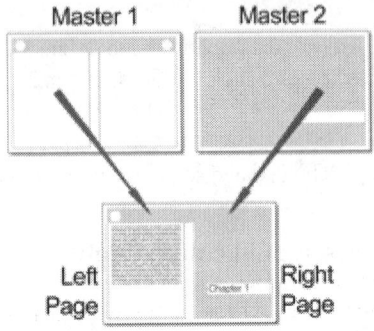

Spread using two dual master pages

Understanding master pages

In PagePlus, single pages are the basic organisational unit, with each page built up using multiple levels and layers, and by **ordering** layout elements in a stack on each layer. If these concepts are new to you, it's important to grasp them (and understand how they are interrelated) in order to tap the full potential of the PagePlus environment.

Master pages

Master pages are part of the structure of your publication, and provide a flexible way to store background elements that you'd like to appear on more than one page—for example a logo, background, header/footer, or border design.

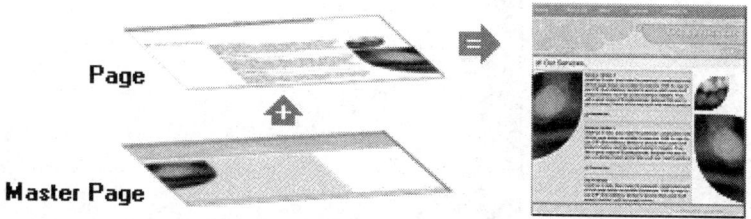

The key concept here is that a particular master page is typically **shared** by multiple pages, as illustrated below. By placing a design element on a master page and then assigning several pages to use that master page, you ensure that all the pages incorporate that element. Of course, each individual page can have its own "foreground" elements.

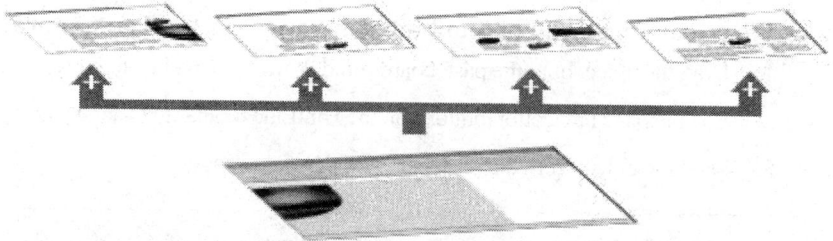

Master pages are available in every publication, but in a simple publication you may not need to use any master pages—or you can get by with just one master page. Facing pages (see p. 25) and multiple master pages prove valuable with longer, more complex documents. Using the **Pages** tab or **Page Manager**, you can quickly add or delete master pages; for example, you could set up different master pages for "title" or "chapter divider" pages. For details, see **Adding, removing, and rearranging pages** on p. 31.

To edit the design elements on a master page, you need to switch the working view to the master page level, as described below.

Viewing pages

Most of the PagePlus display is taken up by a page or "artwork" area and a surrounding "pasteboard" area.

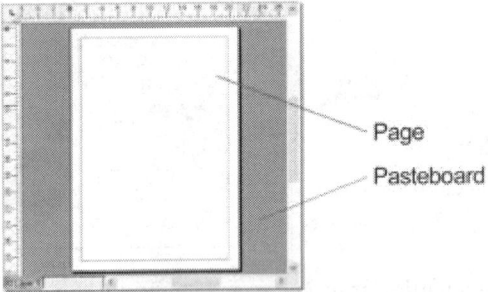

In PagePlus, the **page area** is where you put page layout guides, and of course the text, shapes, and pictures that you want to print. The **pasteboard area** is where you generally keep any text, shapes, or pictures that are being prepared or waiting to be positioned on the page area.

To move or copy an object between pages via the Pasteboard:

1. Drag the object onto the pasteboard (hold down the **Ctrl** key to copy).
2. Use the page navigation buttons on the HintLine toolbar to change pages.
3. Drag the object from the pasteboard onto the new page.

> TIP: An object must be entirely on the pasteboard and not overlapping the page edge!

View controls

PagePlus makes it easy to see exactly what you're working on—from a wide view of multiple pages to a closeup view of a small region. For example, you can use the **scrollbars** at the right and bottom of the main window to move the page and pasteboard with respect to the main window. The view automatically re-enters itself as you drag objects to the edge of the screen. If you're using a **wheel mouse**, you can scroll vertically by rotating the wheel, or horizontally by **Shift**-rotating.

The **View toolbar** at the top of the screen provides the 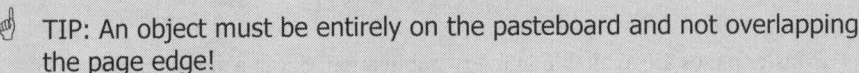 **Pan** tool as an alternative way of moving around, plus a number of buttons that let you zoom in and out so you can inspect and/or edit the page at different levels of detail.

PagePlus 11 User Guide   Working with Pages | 29

If you're using a wheel mouse, you can pan by holding down the wheel while rotating it, or zoom by **Ctrl**-rotating.

You can switch between two viewing modes: **Normal** view, which displays one page at a time, and **Multipage** view, which displays a number of pages at a time in the workspace. In either mode, the pasteboard is shared by all pages. Especially in Normal view, it's useful for copying or moving objects between pages. In Multipage view, it's especially easy to move or copy objects between pages using drag-and-drop. You can easily switch between modes and set the number of pages displayed.

To view multiple pages in the workspace:

1. Click the ⊞ **Multipage View** button on the View toolbar. An array selector appears.

2. Click and drag to choose an array within the selector, for example 2x4 Pages or 3x2 Pages (as shown). To expand the number of choices, drag down and to the right. Click **Normal View** if you change your mind.

The publication appears in Multipage mode with the specified page array in view.

To switch between Normal and Multipage view:

- Choose **Normal** or **Multipage** from the View menu.

In either mode, you can use the ◀ **Previous Page** and ▶ **Next Page** buttons on the HintLine toolbar to step between pages. In Multipage view, you have the additional option of scrolling from one set of pages to the next using the vertical scrollbar or the **Pan** tool.

Navigating

However you choose to structure your publication, PagePlus provides a variety of ways of getting quickly to the elements you need to edit.

To go to a publication page/master page:

1. On the Pages tab, your publication pages appear as thumbnails in the main Pages panel (in page number order).
2. Double-click on a thumbnail in the panel—use the page numbering underneath each thumbnail for navigation. Your selected page is displayed.

For Master pages, click on the **Master Pages ▶** button to expand the Master Pages panel, and double-click on a master page.

Alternatively, you can use the **Page Manager** (View tab) on the HintLine toolbar.

To go to an adjacent page/master page:

- Switch to the level (page or master page) you want to work on, as described **below**, then click the **Previous Page** or **Next Page** button on the HintLine toolbar.

To go to the first or last page/master page:

- Switch to the level (page or master page) you want to work on, as described **below**, then click the **First Page** or **Last Page** button on the HintLine toolbar.

Once you've displayed a page or master page, you can normally edit any object on it—regardless of which layer the object is on—simply by clicking the object. In order to create a new object on a particular layer, you'll first need to "activate" (switch to) that layer.

To switch to a particular layer of a page/master page:

- After displaying the page or master page, click the layer's name in the Layers tab or click to the left of the layer's entry.

The active layer becomes uppermost in the workspace, and a ▶ mark appears next to its entry in the Layers tab.

The master page level

In order to add or edit master page elements, you first need to switch from the regular page level of the publication to the master page level.

To switch between page and master page levels:

- Double-click a thumbnail on the Pages tab to go directly to that page or master page (lower and upper pages, respectively).

Adding, removing, and rearranging pages

Using the **Pages** tab you can quickly rearrange publication pages using drag-and-drop, and add or delete either pages or **master pages** without having to switch to a particular level first. The tab displays Master pages in the collapsible upper panel and standard publication pages in the lower panel.

A Page Manager, accessible from the ▷ **Options** button, provides additional options, such as duplicating a particular page, assigning a specific master page, or adding/deleting multiple pages.

To rearrange pages:

- In the **Pages** tab, drag a page thumbnail in the lower Pages panel to a new place in the panel's page sequence.

To add a single page/master page:

1. On the **Pages** tab, select a page (or master page) by on either panel clicking its thumbnail.

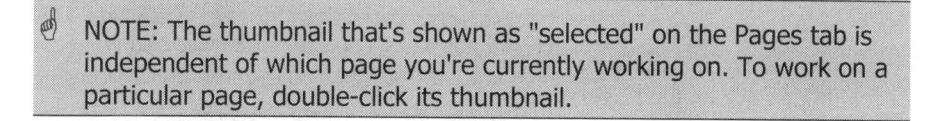

> NOTE: The thumbnail that's shown as "selected" on the Pages tab is independent of which page you're currently working on. To work on a particular page, double-click its thumbnail.

2. To add a page (or master page) **before** the one selected in the panel, click the **Insert Page** button.
   OR
   To add a new page at the end of the publication, first deselect all pages by clicking in the neutral grey region of the lower panel, then click the **Insert Page** button.

A new page added via the Pages tab takes the master page currently selected.

- If there's more than one master page, you can assign a particular master page when creating a new page, by dragging from that master page thumbnail to the neutral region in the lower panel. The new page appears with that master page assigned to its first layer.

To delete a single page/master page:

1. On the **Pages** tab, select the page (or master page) to delete on the appropriate panel by clicking its thumbnail.

2. Click the **Delete Page** button to delete the page.

Working with layers

Each new page or master page consists of a single **layer**. One layer may be enough to accommodate the elements of a particular layout, but you can create additional layers as needed. On each layer, objects such as text frames and pictures are stacked in the order you create them, from back to front, with each new object in front of the others. Layers themselves are stacked in a similar way, and of course you can juggle the order of objects and layers as needed.

Layers are useful when you're working on a complex design where it makes sense to separate one group of objects from another. You can work on one layer at a time without worrying about affecting elements on a different layer.

Once you've displayed a page, you can normally edit any object on it—regardless of which layer the object is on—simply by clicking the object. In order to create a new object on a particular layer, you'll first need to "activate" (switch to) that layer.

Each layer is situated along with other layers (if present) within a stack on the **Layers** tab. The uppermost layer is applied over any lower layer on the page.

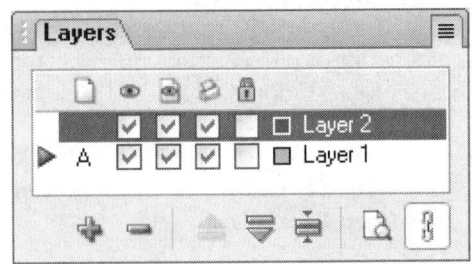

Layer 1 and Layer 2 above could represent the following:

☐ Layer 1   ■ Layer 2   ☐ Layer 1 ■ Layer 2

In order to create a new object on a particular layer, you'll first need to "activate" (switch to) that layer.

To select a particular layer:

- Click (or right-click) a layer name in the **Layers** tab.

> NOTE: Right-clicking a layer name displays a menu of layer-related actions, as well as Options for that particular layer.

To display the Layers tab:

- Go to **View>Studio Tabs** and select the **Layers** tab, if the tab is not visible.

Adding, removing, and rearranging layers

When you **add a new page or master page** to the publication, you can specify whether to copy the layers and/or objects from a particular source page. Once you've created a page, it's easy to add or delete layers as needed.

To add a new layer to the current page or master page:

1. In the Layers tab, click the ![] **Insert** button.
2. You'll be prompted to give the new layer a name and set its **properties**. When you've made your selections, click **OK**.

To delete a layer:

- In the Layers tab, select the layer's name and click the ![] **Delete** button.

You can move layers up or down in the stacking order to place their objects in front or behind those on other layers, move objects to specific layers, and even merge layers.

To move a layer in the stacking order:

- In the Layers tab, select the layer's entry, then click the **Move Up** or **Move Down** button to move the layer up or down in the list, respectively.

To move an object to a specific layer:

- Select the object and choose **Send to Layer** from the Arrange menu, then select the destination layer from the submenu.

To merge one layer with another in the Layers tab:

1. Activate the layer you want to merge **to** by clicking its entry. A ▶ mark indicates that the layer is active.

2. Select the entry of the layer you want to merge, and click the **Merge** button.

The contents of the merged layer appear on the active layer.

Selecting objects on layers

Once you've **displayed a page or master page**, you can normally edit any object on it—regardless of which layer the object is on—simply by clicking the object. In order to select an object on a particular layer, you'll first need to "activate" (switch to) that layer by selecting the layer in the Layers tab.

To select all objects on a particular layer:

- In the Layers tab, right-click the chosen layer and choose **Select All Objects**.

To edit only objects on the active layer:

- In the Layers tab, select the chosen layer and uncheck **Edit all layers**.

Normally the active layer stays the same regardless of which object you select. For ease in identifying which layer a given object resides on, you can set each layer to use a different **selection handle** colour, which is also displayed on the Layers tab. Assigning different handle colours means, for example, that you can quickly verify that a pasted object has gone to the correct layer, i.e. the selection handles of the pasted object would adopt the colour assigned to the layer.

To change a layer's selection handle colour:

1. In the Layers tab, choose the layer.
2. Double-click the box immediately before the layer name.
3. In the Options dialog, click the colour selection button next to **Selection handle**, and choose a colour from the palette (click **More Colours...** for a wider choice).

If you're working with objects on several layers and need to switch quickly to the layer that includes the selected object, PagePlus provides a couple of options.

To activate the layer with the selected object:

1. Select an object whose layer needs to be activated.
2. Choose **Select** from the Edit menu, then choose **Select Layer** from the submenu. You must have the **Edit All layers** button enabled.

OR

- To automatically activate the corresponding layer each time you select an object, check **Autoselect Layer** on the submenu.

Layers and master pages

Master pages are special "background" pages that can be shared by more than one regular page. They are assigned to **each layer** of a regular page rather than to the page as a whole—so if a page has multiple layers it can also employ multiple master pages! For example, one master page might include background text elements, while another included background graphics. By assigning the two master pages to separate layers you could achieve a unified design while keeping the elements separate.

Master 1   Master 2

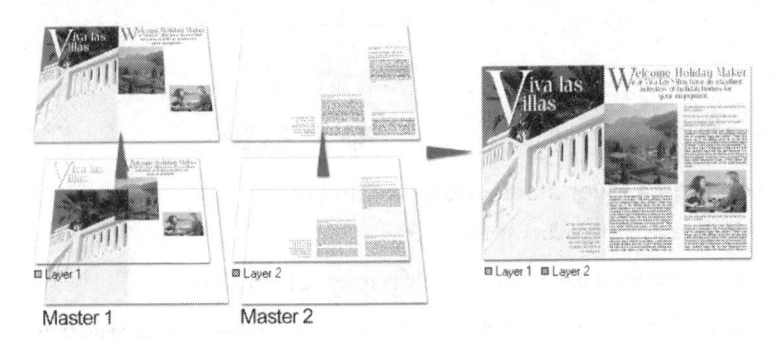

You can also set any layer to use **no master page**. Commonly, the first layer uses a master page while subsequent layers use no master page, but there's no hard and fast rule. You can assign the master page either when you first create the layer, or subsequently, as the layout evolves.

To assign a master page to a page layer:

1. In the Layers tab, double-click in the ▢ **Master Page(s)** column of the chosen page layer.

2. In the **Select Master Page** dialog, select the normal page and master page from the displayed drop-down menus.

Master pages, like regular pages, can have more than one layer. Layers on master pages work almost exactly like those on regular pages. The key difference is that master page layers cannot themselves take a master page; master pages can only be assigned to layers on regular pages.

When you **add a new master page** to the publication, you have the option of copying the layers and/or objects from an existing master page. If you choose not to copy existing layers, the new master page starts out with one layer. You can always add more as described above.

Layer names and properties

The Layers tab and associated Layer Options dialog let you set a variety of properties for one or more layers. It is possible to rename the layer, make the layer and objects on it visible/invisible, assign and view master pages associated with the layer, and lock layers.

To set layer properties:

1. Display the Layers tab.
2. Select desired settings for the layer.

    - Check the box in the ⬜ **Master Page(s)** column to assign a normal and/or master page to the layer.

    - Check the box in the 👁 **Visible** column to show the layer and any objects on it; uncheck to hide the layer.

    - Check the box in the 📄 **Master Page(s) Visible** column to show the layer's master page; uncheck to hide it.

    - Check the 🖨 **Printable** column to include the layer in page printouts; uncheck to exclude it.

    - Check the box in the 🔒 **Locked** column to prevent objects on the layer from being selected/edited; uncheck to allow editing.

    - To set the **Selection handle colour**, click the colour selection button and choose a colour from the palette (click **More Colours...** for a wider choice).

3. If required, you can right-click and view the Layer Options dialog. Here you can extend settings to layers with the same name throughout the publication, check **Apply to all layers with the same name**.

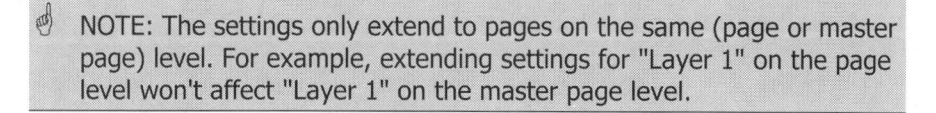

> NOTE: The settings only extend to pages on the same (page or master page) level. For example, extending settings for "Layer 1" on the page level won't affect "Layer 1" on the master page level.

To toggle all layer properties:

- Choose **All Layers Visible**, **All Layers Printable**, or **All Layers Locked** from the View menu.

> NOTE: You can also toggle **View/Master Page Objects** to show/hide master page objects.

The global property **Paste to Source Layer** lets you take advantage of consistent layer naming when pasting from the Clipboard. With the option enabled, PagePlus will paste only to a layer with the same name as that from which objects were copied—i.e. the name of the target layer must match that of the source layer. For example, suppose you've copied an object from the "Body Text" layer on one page.

You can go to another page and simply issue the Paste command to deposit a copy onto that page's "Body Text" layer, saving yourself the preliminary step of activating the correct layer. Again, a bit of forethought when naming your layers will allow you to reap the benefits!

To enable source-layer-only pasting:

- In the Layers tab, go to the **Options** button and select **Paste to Source Layer** from the drop-down menu.

Previewing layers

For a quick view of layer elements in isolation, you can display a thumbnail preview of any layer, with or without its **master page**.

To preview a layer:

- In the Layers tab, select the chosen layer and choose **Preview selected layer**.

PagePlus displays the layer in a preview window. To see the layer minus its master page elements, uncheck **Show master page**.

Setting guides for page margins, rows, columns, and bleeds

Layout guides are visual guide lines that help you position layout elements, either "by eye" or with snapping (see below) turned on. They can include **page margins, row and column guides, bleed area guides**, and/or **ruler guides**.

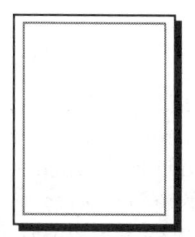

Page margin settings are fundamental to your layout, and usually are among the first choices you'll make after starting a publication from scratch. The page margins are shown as a blue box which is actually four guide lines—for top, bottom, left, and right—indicating the underlying page margin settings. If you like, you can set the margins to match your current printer settings.

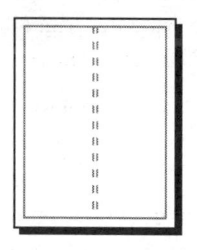

You also have the option of setting up **row** and **column guides** as an underlying layout aid. PagePlus represents rows and columns on the page area with dashed blue guide lines. Unlike the dashed grey **frame margins and columns**, row and column guides don't control where frame text flows. Rather, they serve as visual aids that help you match the frame layout to the desired column layout.

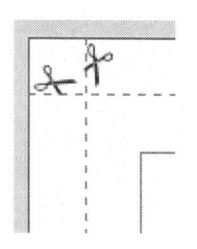

Bleed area guides assist you in positioning "bleed" elements that you want to run to the edge of a trimmed page. To allow for inaccuracies in the trimming process in professional printing, it's a good idea to extend these elements beyond the "trim edge"—the dimensions defined by your Page Setup. With bleed guides switched on, the page border expands by a distance you specify, and the trim edge is shown with dashed lines and little "scissors" symbols. Note that these guide lines are just a visual aid; only the Bleed limit setting in the Print dialog extends the actual output page size.

Defining layout guides

To define layout guides:

- Choose [Layout Guides] on the Page context bar. Then use the Margins tab as described below.

The **Margins** tab lets you set guide lines for page margins, rows, and columns. You can set the left, right, top, and bottom margins individually, or click the **From Printer** button to derive the page margin settings from the current printer settings. The dialog also provides options for **balanced margins** (left matching right, top matching bottom) or for two **mirrored margins** on facing pages where the "left" margin setting becomes the "inside," and the "right" margin becomes the "outside." (See **Facing pages** on p. 25.)

Use the **Row and Column Guides** section to define guides for rows and columns. If you want rows or columns of uneven width, first place them at fixed intervals, then later drag on the guides to reposition them as required.

Use the **Bleed Area Guides** section to specify the extra margin you want to allow around the original Page Setup dimensions or "trim area". Note that if the setting is zero or you have **View>Bleed Area Guides** unchecked, you won't see the bleed area displayed.

To show or hide layout guides you've defined:

- Check or uncheck **Guide Lines** on the View menu.

This setting also affects any ruler guides you've placed on the page area. It doesn't affect display of bleed area guides (see below).

To switch bleed area display on or off:

- Check or uncheck **Bleed Area Guides** on the View menu.

Using the rulers and dot grid

The PagePlus **rulers** mimic the paste-up artist's T-square, and serve several purposes:

- To act as a measuring tool
- To set and display tab stops
- To set and display paragraph indents
- To create ruler guides for aligning and snapping

Ruler units

To select the basic measurement unit used by the rulers:

- Choose **Options...** from the Tools menu and select the **Rulers** page.

In Paper Publishing mode, the default unit is inches or centimetres; in Web Publishing mode, the default is pixels.

Adjusting rulers

By default, the horizontal ruler lies along the top of the PagePlus window and the vertical ruler along the left edge. The default **ruler intersection** is the top left corner of the pasteboard area. The default **zero point** (marked as 0 on each ruler) is the top left corner of the page area. (Even if you have set up **bleed area guides** and the screen shows an oversize page, the zero point stays in the same place, i.e. the top left corner of the trimmed page.)

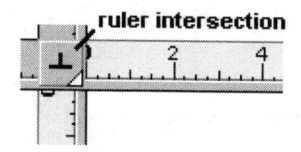

To define a new zero point:

- Drag the arrow on the ruler intersection to the new zero point on the page or pasteboard. (Be sure to click only the arrow—the intersection button is also used for setting tab stops!)

To move the rulers:

- With the **Shift** key down, drag the arrow on the ruler intersection. The zero point remains unchanged.

- Double-click on the ruler intersection to make the rulers and zero point jump to the top left-hand corner of the currently selected object. This comes in handy for measuring page objects.

To restore the original ruler position and zero point:

- Double-click the arrow on the ruler intersection.

To lock the rulers and prevent them from being moved:

- Choose **Tools>Options...** and select the **Rulers** page, then check **Lock Rulers**.

Rulers as a measuring tool

The most obvious role for rulers is as a measuring tool. As you move the mouse pointer, small lines along each ruler display the current horizontal and vertical cursor position. When you click to select an object, white ruler regions indicate the object's left, right, top, and bottom edges. Each region has a zero point relative to the object's upper left corner, so you can see the object's dimensions at a glance.

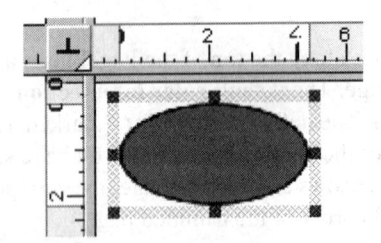

Creating ruler guides

PagePlus lets you to set up horizontal and vertical **ruler guides**—non-printing, red lines you can use to align headlines, pictures, and other layout elements.

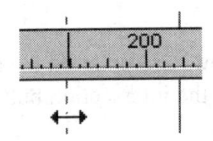

- To create a ruler guide, click on a ruler. The red ruler guide line appears.
- To move a guide, drag it.
- To remove a guide, drag and drop it anywhere outside the page area.

- To lock ruler guides, choose **Tools>Options...** and select the **Rulers** page, then check **Lock Ruler Guides**.

- To fine-position ruler guides, choose **Layout Guides...** from the File menu (or right-click menu) and select the **Ruler** tab. You can use the tab to create or delete individual guides. To delete all ruler guides at once, click the **Clear All** button.

Using the dot grid

The **dot grid** is a matrix of dots or lines based on ruler units, covering the page and pasteboard areas. Like ruler guides, it's handy for both visual alignment and snapping.

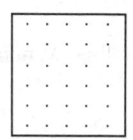

- To turn the dot grid on and off, check (or uncheck) **Dot Grid** on the View menu.
  OR:
  Choose **Options...** from the Tools menu and display the **Layout** page. Check or uncheck **Dot Grid**.

You can set the grid spacing, style, and colour in the Options dialog.

To change the grid spacing, style, and/or colour:

1. Choose **Options...** from the Tools menu and display the **Layout** page.
2. To set the grid interval, enter a value in the "Grid lines" box.
3. To display the grid using dots, select "Dots" in the "Grid" option. To display grid lines or crosses, select "Solid" or "Crosses", respectively.
4. To change the colour of grid dots, click the **Colour** button and then select a colour thumbnail.

Snapping

The **snapping** feature simplifies placement and alignment by "magnetising" grid dots and guide lines. When snapping is on, the edges and centres of objects you create, move, or resize will jump to align with the nearest visible **grid dot** or **guides**. Objects normally snap to the page edge, too.

Guide lines include ruler guides as well as layout guide lines based on page margins, rows, columns, and bleeds (see **Setting guides for page margins, rows, columns, and bleeds** on p. 39). Check or uncheck **Guide Lines** on the View menu to switch guides on or off.

To turn snapping on and off:

- Click the ![icon] **Snapping** button on the HintLine toolbar. When the button is down, snapping is on.

Selective snapping

You control which points and lines are snapped to by showing or hiding the individual guide elements (i.e., Rulers, Guide lines, Frames, Dot Grid, etc.), and by changing options settings for those visible elements.

To show or hide guide elements:

- Check (or uncheck) the element's name on the **View** or menu.
  OR
  Right-click on the page or pasteboard and choose **View**, then select the element's name.

To set which visible elements are snapped to:

1. Choose **Options...** from the Tools menu.
2. Under "Snap to:" on the Layout tab, uncheck any elements you don't want to snap to. The choices include **Grid dots**, **Page/Bleed edge**, **Page margins**, **Ruler guides**, **Row/column guides** and **Nearest Pixel**.

Using headers and footers

Headers and footers are layout elements that go at the top and bottom (respectively) of your master page(s), and are repeated on every page of your publication. The Headers and Footers Wizard lets you create these elements easily. (See also **Inserting footnotes and endnotes** on p. 88.)

To create headers and/or footers:

- Choose **Headers & Footers...** from the Insert menu, and follow the Wizard instructions.

To edit existing headers and footers, or create more complex master page elements:

- Switch to the master page layer by clicking the Current Page box on the HintLine toolbar (or to simply edit them, you can rerun the Wizard).

Using page numbering

Page number fields automatically display the current page number. Typically, page number fields are used on the **master page** level so they will appear on every page, but you can insert a page number field anywhere in your text. You can change the style of page numbers, and the page on which numbering first appears.

To define a header or footer that includes page number fields:

- Choose **Headers & Footers...** from the Insert menu.

To insert a page number field:

1. In Paper Publishing mode, switch to the master page layer (if desired) by clicking the Current Page box on the HintLine toolbar.
2. Create a new text object if necessary. Click for an insertion point where you want to place the page number field.
3. Choose **Page Number** from the Insert menu.

To change page numbering style:

- Choose **Page Number Format...** from the Format menu.

You can select from standard numbering schemes such as Arabic numerals (1, 2, 3...) or Upper Roman (I, II, III...). You can also specify the **First Page Number** in the sequence (this will appear on the first publication page). For example, Chapter Two of a long publication might be in a separate file and begin numbering with page 33.

Updating and saving defaults

Object defaults are the stored property settings PagePlus applies to newly created text, graphics, and frames. When you create text in your publication, it will have default properties for font, size, colour, alignment, etc. New graphics will have default properties for line and fill colour, shade, pattern, etc. New frames will have default properties for margins, columns, etc. You can easily change the defaults for any type of object.

Default settings are always **local**—that is, any changed defaults apply to the current publication and are automatically saved with it, so they're in effect next time you open that publication. However, at any time you can use the Save Defaults command to record the current defaults as **global** settings that will be in effect for any new publication you subsequently create.

To set local defaults for a particular type of object:

1. Create a single sample object and fine-tune its properties as desired—or use an existing object that already has the right properties. (For graphics, you can use a line, shape, or rectangle; all share the same set of defaults.)

2. Select the object that's the basis for the new defaults and choose **Update Object Default** from the Format menu.
   OR
   Right-click the sample object and choose **Format>Update Object Default**.

You can also view and change the current default text properties in the Text Style Palette.

To view and change default text properties:

1. Choose **Text Style Palette...** from the Format menu.

2. Click **Default Text**, then click **Modify...** to view current settings.

3. Use the **Attributes** button to alter character, paragraph, or other properties.

To save all current defaults as global settings:

1. Choose **Save Defaults** from the Tools menu.

2. Click **OK** to confirm that you want new publications to use the current publication's defaults.

Setting PagePlus options

The **Options dialog** lets you customise a wide range of PagePlus preference settings, including picture and layout options, ease-of-use features, and so on. As a rule, Options settings are global—that is, changing them affects all open publications, and when you close PagePlus, your current Options settings remain in effect the next time you open the program.

To set PagePlus options:

1. Choose **Options...** from the Tools menu.
2. Use the branching menu to display one of the dialog pages, and then set your options.

Working with Objects

4

What are Objects?

Objects are considered to be any text, shape, line, box, or image that exist on your publication page. They can be manipulated with respect to their size, position, grouping and orientation.

Selecting an object

Before you can change any object, you need to select it using one of these tools from the Tools menu:

Pointer tool
Click to use the **Pointer tool** to select, move, copy, and resize objects.

Rotate tool
Click to use the **Rotate tool** to rotate an object around its top left handle. Select the object, then drag one of its handles. You can also use the Rotate tool to move and copy objects. See **Rotating an object** on p. 63.

Square Crop and Irregular Crop tools
Choose either **Crop tool** from the Crop flyout to crop (or trim) objects. Select the object, then drag one of its handles inward. You can also use a Crop tool to move and copy objects. See **Cropping and combining objects** on p. 64.

To select an object:

- Click on the object using one of the tools shown above. A grey bounding box appears, with small "handles" appear defining the object's corners and edges.

- If objects overlap, click with the **Alt** key down until the desired object is selected.

When selecting a text object with the Pointer tool:

- Clicking on a text object with the Pointer tool selects the object and also positions the blinking text selection cursor within the object's text. In this mode, you can edit the text.

- Double-click to select a word, and triple-click to select a paragraph.

- Press the **Delete** key to delete characters after the cursor. To delete the frame itself, choose **Delete Object** from the Edit menu.

To select only the frame (for example, to adjust its margin and column guides), click the frame's bounding box.

Ruler regions

When you click to select an object, white ruler regions indicate the left, right, top, and bottom edges of the object.

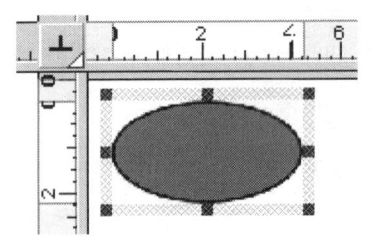

For details on using the rulers, see **Using the rulers** on p. 41.

Selecting multiple objects

Selecting more than one object at a time (creating a **multiple selection**) lets you:

- Position or resize all the objects at the same time.

- Create a **group object** from the multiple selection, which can then be treated as a single object, with the option of restoring the individual objects later. See **Creating Groups** on p. 53.

To create a multiple selection:

- Click in a blank area of the page and drag a "marquee" box around the objects you want to select. Repeated **Shift**-drags add to the selection region.
  OR
  Hold down the **Shift** key and click each object in turn.

To add or remove an object from a multiple selection:

- Hold down the **Shift** key and click the object to be added or removed.

To deselect all objects in a multiple selection:

- Click in a blank area of the page.

To select all objects on the page (or master page):

- Choose **Select All** from the Edit menu (or press **Ctrl+A**).

To select all objects of one type on the page (or master page):

- Hold down the **Ctrl** key and double-click one object of that type.

To select all objects on a layer:

- Display the Layers tab, choose the layer name and right-click to select the **Select All Objects** button.

Creating groups

You can easily turn a **multiple selection** into a group object. When objects are grouped, you can position, resize, or rotate the objects all at the same time.

Simply clicking on any member of a **group** selects the group object. In general, any operation you carry out on a selected group affects each member of the group. However, you can also select and edit an individual object within a group.

To create a group from a multiple selection:

- Click the ![] **Group** button below the selection.

To ungroup:

- Click the ![] **Ungroup** button below the selection to turn back to a multiple selection.

Simply clicking on any member of a group selects the group object. In general, any operation you carry out on a selected group affects each member of the group. However, the objects that comprise a group are intact, and you can also select and edit an individual object within a group.

To select an individual object within a group:

- **Ctrl**-click the object.

Copying, pasting, and duplicating objects

Besides using the Windows Clipboard to copy and paste objects, you can duplicate objects easily using drag-and-drop, and **replicate** multiple copies of any object in precise formations. You can also **transfer the formatting** of one object to another, with the option of selecting specific attributes to be included when formatting is pasted.

To copy an object (or multiple selection) to the Windows Clipboard:

- Click the ![] **Copy** button on the Standard toolbar.

If you're using another Windows application, you can usually copy and paste objects via the Clipboard.

To paste an object from the Clipboard:

- Click the **Paste** button on the Standard toolbar.

The standard Paste command inserts the object at the insertion point or (for a separate object) at the centre of the page. To insert a separate object at the same page location as the copied item, use the **Paste in Place** command (**Ctrl+Alt+V**).

To choose between alternative Clipboard formats:

- Choose **Paste Special...** from the Edit menu.

To duplicate an object:

1. Select the object, then press the **Ctrl** key. The cursor changes to the Copy cursor.
2. Drag the outline to a new location on the page. You can release the **Ctrl** key once you've started the drag.
3. To constrain the position of the copy (to same horizontal or vertical), press and hold down the **Shift** key while dragging. A duplicate of the object appears at the new location.

Replicating objects

Duplicating an object means making just one copy at a time. The **Replicate** command lets you create multiple copies in a single step, with precise control over how the copies are arranged, either as a linear series or a grid. You can include one or more transformations to produce an interesting array of rotated and/or resized objects. It's great for repeating backgrounds, or for perfectly-aligned montages of an image or object.

To replicate an object:

1. Select the object to be replicated and choose **Replicate...** from the Edit menu. The Replicate dialog appears, with a preview region at the right.

2. To arrange copies in a straight line, select **Create line**. For an X-by-Y grid arrangement, select **Create grid**.

3. Specify **Line length** (the number of objects including the original) in the arrangement, or the Grid size. Note that you can use the Line length setting to include an odd number of objects in a grid.

4. Set spacing between the objects as either an **Offset** (measured between the top left corners of successive objects) or a **Gap** (between the bottom right and top left corners). You can specify **Horizontal** and/or **Vertical** spacing, and/or an angular **Rotation**. To set a specific horizontal or vertical interval, check **Absolute**; uncheck the box to specify the interval as a percentage of the original object's dimensions.

5. Click **OK**.

The result is a multiple selection. Click its **Group** button if you want to keep the separate objects linked for additional manipulations.

Pasting an object's formatting

Once you have copied an object to the Clipboard, you can use the **Paste Format** to apply its formatting attributes to another object. **Paste Format Plus** displays a "master control" dialog that lets you select or deselect specific attributes to be included when formatting is pasted. See the PagePlus Help for more information on the Paste Format Plus feature.

To paste one object's formatting to another:

1. Copy the source object.

2. Select the target object and choose **Paste Format** from the Edit menu (or press **Ctrl+Shift+V**).

The target object takes on any formatting attributes and settings of the source object that are currently defined in Paste Format Plus.

Moving objects

To move an object (including a multiple selection):

- Click within the object (not on a handle) and drag it to the new location while holding down the left mouse button (excludes frames).
  OR
  Drag the object's grey bounding box.

The view automatically re-centres itself as you drag objects to the edge of the screen.

> **TIP:** In Multipage view, you can drag and drop objects between pages. Use the **Multipage** button on the View toolbar to set up a convenient viewing mode.

To constrain the movement of an object to horizontal or vertical:

- Select the object and use the keyboard arrows (up, down, left, right).
  OR
  Press and hold down the **Shift** key after you begin dragging the object.

Release the **Shift** key after you release the left mouse button.

Specifying object positions with the Transform tab

The Transform tab includes controls for fine-tuning the position of a selected object:

X **Horizontal position**
Changes the horizontal placement of the object's top left corner, with respect to the ruler's zero point. The higher the value, the further to the right.

Y **Vertical position**
Changes the vertical placement of the object's top left corner, with respect to the ruler's zero point. The higher the value, the lower on the page.

Resizing objects

PagePlus provides several methods of resizing objects. Click-and-drag is the simplest—watch the HintLine for context-sensitive tips and shortcuts! For extremely precise resizing, use the Transform tab.

> **TIP:** To set two or more objects to the same horizontal or vertical size as the last selected object, you can use **Arrange/Size Objects....**

To resize an object (in general):
1. Select the object.
2. Click one of the object's handles and drag it to a new position while holding down the left mouse button.

Dragging from an edge handle resizes in one dimension, by moving that edge. Dragging from a corner handle resizes in two dimensions, by moving two edges. You can also constrain the resizing—note that pictures normally behave differently from lines, shapes, and text objects.

Resizing lines, shapes, artistic text, frame objects, and table objects

Text in frames and tables doesn't change size when the container object is resized.

To resize freely:
- Drag from a corner (or line end) handle.

To constrain a shape, frame object, or table object when resizing:
- Hold the **Shift** key down and drag from a corner (or line end) handle.

Resizing pictures

These objects are normally constrained when resized, since you'll typically want to preserve their proportions.

To resize while maintaining aspect ratio (proportions):
- Drag from a corner handle.

To resize freely:
- Hold the **Shift** key down and drag from a corner handle.

To adjust picture size and/or resolution:

1. Select the picture and click the **Resize Picture** button on the Picture context bar (only shown when an image is selected). The Picture Size & Resolution dialog appears.
2. Set a Width, Height and Horizontal/Vertical resolution for your picture. Rescale your picture if needed.

Resizing groups

You can resize a group object. The size of images, graphic objects, and text objects in the group will change. The size of text inside frames or tables won't change, only the size of the text container.

> NOTE: You can move, but cannot resize, a multiple selection. Turn the multiple selection into a group first, by clicking the **Group** button below the selection.

Specifying object dimensions with the Transform tab

The Transform tab includes controls for fine-tuning the dimensions of a selected object:

W **Object width**
Move the object's right edge with respect to its left edge. The left edge stays the same.

H **Object height**
Move the object's bottom edge with respect to its top edge. The top edge stays the same.

% **Scale Width**
Change the width of the selected object with respect to its left edge, as a percentage.

% **Scale Height**
Change the height of the selected object with respect to its top edge, as a percentage.

Setting the size of an imported or pasted picture

When using the **Import Picture** or **Paste Special...** command, after you select the required picture format, the mouse pointer changes to the **Picture Paste** cursor. What you do next determines the initial size and placement of the image:

- To insert the picture at a default size, simply click the mouse.
  OR
  To set the picture size, drag out a region and release the mouse button.

When you click to paste in a picture, you can tell in advance what size PagePlus thinks the picture should be—white regions appear in the rulers.

Locking an object's size or position

To prevent accidentally moving, resizing, flipping, or rotating an object, you can lock it in position.

To lock/unlock an object:

Right-click on the object and check or uncheck **Arrange>Lock Objects**.

Arranging Objects

Each new page or master page consists of a single **layer**. One layer may be enough to accommodate the elements of a particular layout, but you can **create additional layers** as needed. On each layer, objects such as text frames and pictures are **stacked** in the order you create them, from back to front, with each new object in front of the others. You can change the stacking order, which affects how objects appear on the page.

To change the object's position in the stacking order:

- To shift the selected object's position to the bottom layer, use the **Send to Back** button on the Arrange toolbar.

- To shift the selected object's position to the top layer, use the **Bring to Front** button on the Arrange toolbar.

- To shift the object's position one layer toward the front, right-click on the object and choose **Arrange>Forward One**.

- To shift the object's position one layer toward the back, right-click on the object and choose **Arrange>Back One**.

Aligning and distributing objects

Precise **alignment** is one key to a professional layout. You can align the edges of any two or more objects with one another, space them out at certain intervals, or align objects with a page margin. In addition, layout tools such as **rulers** and the **dot grid** provide guides to assist you in placing objects on the page. **Snapping** lets you align objects with nearby guides.

The **Align** tab aligns the edges of any two or more objects with one another, space them out at certain intervals, or align objects with a page margin.

Top
Aligns selected objects to the top of the page.

Bottom
Aligns selected objects to the bottom of the page.

Left
Aligns selected objects to their left edges.

Right
Aligns selected objects to their right edges.

Vertical Centre
Aligns selected objects vertically to their centres.

Horizontal Centre
Aligns selected objects horizontally to their centres.

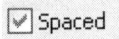

Spaced
Check to enable spacing of distributed objects then use the adjacent box to set a point size by which objects are to be spaced. If unchecked objects are spread across the page.

Distributed Vertical
Spreads the selected objects vertically either across the whole page or by a set amount of spacing (see Spaced).

Distributed Horizontal
Spreads the selected objects horizontally either across the whole page or by a set amount of spacing (see Spaced).

Check to align the selected objects with the page margins.

To align the edges of two or more objects:

1. Using the Pointer tool, **Shift**-click on all the objects you want to align, or draw a marquee box around them, to create a multiple selection.
2. Select the **Align tab**.
3. In the Align tab or dialog, select an option for vertical and/or horizontal alignment. Choose **Top, Bottom, Left, Right, Vertical Centre** or **Horizontal Centre**.
4. Alternatively, to distribute the objects, you can choose **Distributed Horizontal** or **Distributed Vertical** to spread selected objects uniformly across the either the whole page or by a set measurement (check Spaced and set a value in any measurement unit).

To align one or more objects with the page margins:

- Follow the steps above, but check **Include margins**. (If only one object is selected, the option is checked by default.)

Converting an object to a picture

The **Convert To Picture** function deletes the selected object or group and replaces it with an embedded picture representation. It has many practical uses, for example:

- Combining objects into a permanent graphic, such as a logo created from multiple text, graphic, and picture objects. The resulting graphic can then be sized, positioned, and rotated as a single object.
- Creating a composite shape from multiple graphics.
- Specifying a preferred image format for a particular need, for example to minimize file size or optimise Web quality.

You can select from common bitmap image formats, e.g., .PNG, .JPG or .GIF. (For details on image formats, see **Importing images** and **Setting Web picture display options** on p. 131 or 225, respectively.)

To convert one or more objects to a picture:

1. Select the object or **Shift**-click (or drag a marquee) to select multiple objects.
2. Choose **Convert To Picture...** from the Tools or right-click menu.
3. For bitmap output, choose a specific image format from the list. To specify settings such as compression or transparency, click the **Settings** button.
4. Click **OK**.

Exporting as a picture

Exporting as a picture lets you convert all the objects on the pasteboard and page, or just the currently selected object(s), to an image file, using a file format you specify. It's particularly useful for generating logos and pictures to be used in publications created in other applications, such as a word processor.

To export as a picture:

1. (If exporting objects, not the whole page) Select the object or **Shift**-click (or drag a marquee) to select multiple objects.
2. Choose **Export As Picture...** from the File menu.
3. In the "Save as type" box, select an image file format.
4. Specify a folder and file name for the picture.
5. To export just selected object(s), check **Selected object(s)**. To export the whole page, uncheck this box.
6. To choose from export options such as resolution, colour, and transparency, check **Show Filter Options**.
7. Click **Save**. You'll see export options, if available and requested, for the particular export filter in use.

Rotating an object

You can rotate objects, including text objects and groups. (You cannot rotate a multiple selection.)

To rotate an object:

1. Select the **Rotate tool** on the Tools toolbar.
2. Click to select the object, hover over one of its handles until you see the rotate pointer (below).

3. Hold the mouse button down and drag the pointer in the direction in which you want to rotate the object, then release (use Shift key for 15° rotation intervals).

To unrotate (restore the original orientation):

- Double-click the object.
- To restore the rotated position, double-click again.

To rotate an object 90 degrees left or right:

- Select the object and click the **Rotate Left** or **Rotate Right** button on the Standard toolbar.

To fine-tune rotation:

1. Display the Transform tab. Using the **Object rotation** control...
2. Click the right arrow and drag the slider to accurately adjust rotation.
   OR
   Click the small up or down "nudge" buttons to adjust in 1° increments.
   OR
   Click in the text box, then press the up or down arrows on the keyboard to adjust values incrementally.
   OR
   Type in an exact value and press the **Enter** key.

To prevent a picture object from accidentally being rotated:

- Right-click on the object and check **Arrange>Lock Objects**.

Flipping an object

You can flip objects horizontally (left to right; top and bottom stay the same) or vertically (top to bottom; left and right stay the same).

To flip an object horizontally/vertically:

- Select the object and choose **Flip Horizontal** or **Flip Vertical** from the Arrange menu.

To prevent an object from accidentally being flipped:

- Right-click on the object and check **Arrange>Lock Objects**.

Cropping and combining objects

Cropping means masking (hiding) parts of an object or group, for example to improve composition or create a special effect. The underlying object is intact. You can use either the **Square** or **Irregular Crop** tool to adjust the object's crop outline. You can use either Crop tool to select, move, or copy objects. You can even rotate a cropped object or crop a rotated object.

Still another cropping option is the **Crop to Shape** command, which lets you crop one object to the outline of another.

Objects other than inline pictures have a **wrap outline** which determines how text flows around the object. You can adjust this independently of the crop outline.

The **Combine Curves** command, like Crop to Shape, starts with more than one object, but creates a special composite object with one or more "holes" on the inside where the component objects' fills overlapped one another—useful for creating mask or stencil effects.

To crop using the object's original outline:

1. Select the ⊡ **Square Crop** tool on the Tools toolbar's Crop flyout.
2. Click to select the object or group, then drag one of its edge or corner handles inward. Press the **Shift** key for free (unconstrained) cropping.

To crop by modifying the object's outline:

- Select the object and select the ⊠ **Irregular Crop** tool on the Tools toolbar's Crop flyout. The Curve context bar appears, and you'll see the nodes and connecting segments that define the object's crop outline.

- To move a node (control point) where you see the cursor, drag the node.

- To move a line segment (between two nodes) where you see the cursor, drag the segment.

- To convert an outline from straight lines to curves, click the **Fit Curves** button on the Curve context bar.

- To adjust the curvature of a segment, drag the control handle(s) of the adjacent nodes.

- To add or delete nodes for more or less complex outlines, select a node and click the **Add Node** or **Delete Node** button on the Curve context bar.

- To move the object relative to its crop outline, drag its interior when you see the hand cursor.

To scroll the visible portion of a cropped object within the crop area:

- Select the object and drag its centre area.

To uncrop (restore full visibility):

- Click the **Remove Crop** button on the Tools toolbar's Crop flyout.

Cropping one shape to another

The **Crop to Shape** command works with exactly two objects selected. Either or both of these may be a group object. The lower object (the one behind the other) gets clipped to the outline of the upper object, leaving a shape equivalent to the overlapping region. Note that you can't crop a **mesh-warped object**, but can use one to crop another object. Use **Combine Curves** to use one shape to punch a "hole" in another.

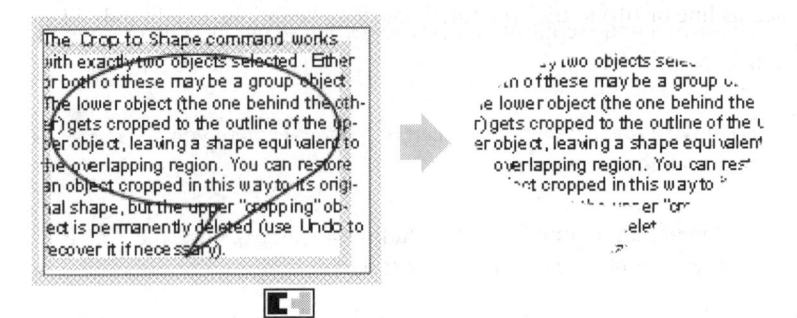

To crop one shape to another:

1. Place the "clipping" object in front of the object to be cropped, using the Arrange menu and/or Arrange toolbar as needed. In the illustration above, a QuickShape is in front of a text frame.

2. Choose **Crop to Shape** from the Tools menu.

You can restore an object cropped in this way to its original shape, but the upper "cropping" object is permanently deleted (use **Undo** to recover it if necessary).

Cropping to the wrap outline

Objects other than inline pictures have a **wrap outline** which determines how text flow changes if the object overlaps a text frame. Initially the wrap outline is set to match the crop outline, but for adjustment purposes the two are independent unless you specify that the crop outline should match the wrap outline. If you're planning to wrap text around an object and also need to crop it somewhat, it will save effort to adjust the wrap outline first, then set the crop outline to match.

To crop a selected object to its wrap outline:

1. Click the **Wrap Settings...** button on the Arrange toolbar.

2. Check the Crop object to wrap outline box.

For details, see **Wrapping text to an object** on p. 94.

Combining lines and shapes

Combining curves is a way of creating a composite object from two or more lines or drawn shapes. As with cropping to a shape, the object in front clips the object(s) behind, in this case leaving one or more "holes" where the component objects overlapped. As with **grouping**, you can apply formatting (such as line or fill) to the combined object and continue to edit individual nodes and segments with the Pointer tool. Unlike those other methods, a combined object will permanently take the line and fill properties of the first selected object.

Combining is a quick way to create a mask or stencil cutout:

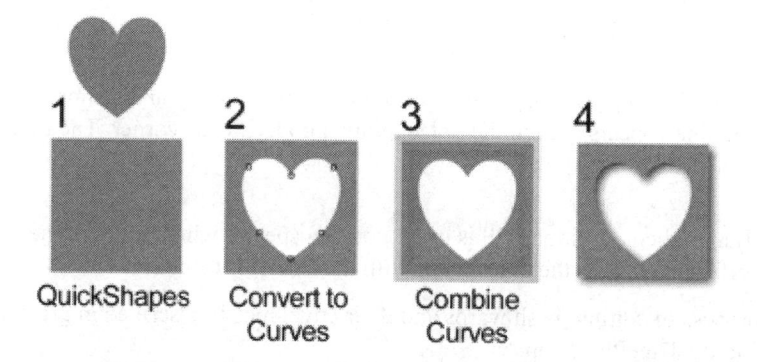

| 1 QuickShapes | 2 Convert to Curves | 3 Combine Curves | 4 |

To combine two or more selected lines or drawn QuickShapes:

1. Draw your two lines or QuickShapes.
2. Place the "clipping" object in front of the object to be cut out, using the Arrange menu and/or Arrange toolbar as needed.
3. Select each object and choose **Tools>Convert to Curves** for both.
4. Group both objects.
5. Choose **Combine Curves** from the Arrange menu.

To restore the original shapes from a combined object:

- Select it and choose **Split Curves** from the Arrange menu.

Applying a mesh warp envelope

Mesh warping lets you define a flexible grid of points and lines that you can drag to deform or distort an object and (optionally) its fill. After applying a basic mesh warp envelope from the **Mesh Warp flyout**, you can use the **Mesh Warp** toolbar to edit the mesh by varying its curvature. You can even custom-design a mesh to match a particular object's geometry—for example, curves that follow the facial contours in a bitmap image—for more precise control of the warp effect. The effect is removable and doesn't permanently alter the object. Note that you can't crop a mesh-warped object, but can use one to crop another object (see **Cropping and combining objects** on p. 64.).

To apply a basic mesh warp to a selected object:

- Click the ⊠ **Mesh Warp** button on the Attributes toolbar and choose a preset warp envelope from the flyout.

warp ⊠ ➡ **warp**

When you first apply a warp, the object deforms accordingly and a simple mesh outline appears around the object, with a node at each corner. The Mesh toolbar also appears.

If a gradient or bitmap fill is used, you can specify whether or not the warp effect extends to the object's fill with the **Warp Fills** button.

The process of editing mesh warps and their envelopes is described in greater detail in the PagePlus Help.

Working with Text

5

Importing text from a file

Importing text from a word-processor file is the traditional way to create text content for Desktop Publishing layouts (but you can also create a story using WritePlus). If you use your current word processor (such as Microsoft Word) to create the text file for your publication, you can import any number of files into one publication. Each file becomes a **story** consisting of a self-contained section of text like a single article in a newspaper, which resides in one or more linked **text frames**.

> TIP: PagePlus will preserve the formatting of imported word-processor text. However, if you're using your word processor to create text specifically for PagePlus, you'll save time by typing as text only, and applying formatting later in PagePlus.

To import text:

1. Choose **Text File...** from the Insert menu, or right-click an existing frame and choose **Text File....** The **Open** dialog appears.

2. Select the format of the source file to be imported and locate the file itself. (See below for details on setting the preferred text import format.)

3. Check the "Retain Format" box to retain the source file's formatting styles. Uncheck the box to discard this information. In either case, PagePlus will preserve basic character properties like italic, bold, and underline, and paragraph properties like alignment (left, centre, right).
   For details on how PagePlus handles text styles, see **Using text styles** on p. 89.

4. Check the "Ignore Line Wrapping" box to ignore returns in the source text— that is, only if the file has been saved with a carriage return at the end of every line, and you want to strip off these extra returns. Otherwise, leave the box unchecked.

5. Click **OK**.

PagePlus will import the designated text into the preselected text object or a new text frame.

Setting the preferred text import format

PagePlus supports direct text import from a number of major word processing applications. Direct import means that in order to import files of a particular format, the word processing application itself must be present on your machine. During installation, PagePlus checks for an installed word processor. You can change the preferred setting to any of the supported applications.

To designate the preferred text import format:

1. Choose **Options...** from the Tools menu.
2. On the **General** page, select your preferred word processor in the "Import text using" drop-down list.

If you find that PagePlus does not list your word processor, or if text import from the designated application fails, choose the "Standard Converters" setting, which provides additional formats.

Understanding text frames

Typically, text in PagePlus goes into **text frames**, which work equally well as containers for single words, standalone paragraphs, or multipage articles or chapter text. You can also use **artistic text** (see p. 78) for standalone text with special effects, or **table text** (see **Creating text-based tables** on p. 107) for row-and-column displays.

What's a text frame?

A text frame is effectively a mini-page, with:

- Margins and column guides to control text flow
- Optional preceding and following frames
- Text and optional **inline images** that flow through the frame (from the previous frame and on to the next).

The text in a frame is called a **story**.

- When you move a text frame, its story text moves with it.
- When you resize a text frame, its story text reflows to the new dimensions.

Frames can be linked so that a single story continues from one frame to another. But text frames can just as easily stand alone. Thus in any publication, you can create text in a single frame, spread a story over several frames, and/or include many independent frame sequences. By placing text frames anywhere, in any order, you can build up newspaper or newsletter style publications with many stories flowing from one page to another.

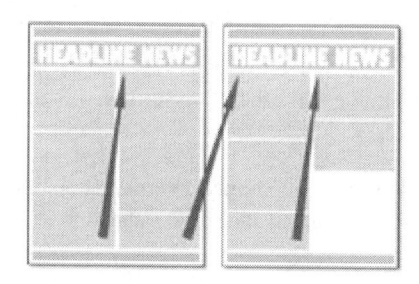

When you select a frame you'll see its bounding box, indicated by a grey border line plus corner and edge handles, and (if you clicked with the Pointer tool) a blinking insertion point in the frame's text. In this mode, you can edit the text with the Pointer tool. As in a word processor, double-clicking selects a word, and triple-clicking selects a paragraph. (For details, see **Editing text on the page** on p. 83.)

Text frames behave like other PagePlus objects—you can resize, move, and even crop or rotate them. You can also apply line, fill, and transparency properties to frames. For some operations, it's more convenient if you get rid of the text insertion point and select only the frame.

To select only the frame (no insertion point):

- Click the frame's bounding box.

When only the frame is selected, you can move it more easily. And only in this mode can you directly adjust the frame **margin and column guides** (which constrain the flow of text), as described in **Frame setup and layout** below.

To move a text frame:

- Drag the frame's bounding box.
  OR
  Use the X or Y options in the Transform tab.

To resize a text frame:

- In any selection mode, drag a corner or edge handle.
  OR
  Use the W or H options in the Transform tab.

Creating frames

You add frames to a page as you would any other object. PagePlus supports a wide variety of frame shapes. You can resize any frame, but cannot alter its basic shape.

To create a frame:

1. For a standard (rectangular) frame, click the **Standard Frame** button.
   OR
   For an irregular frame, click the **Shaped Frame** button (its icon will display the most recently selected shape) and select a shape from the flyout submenu.
2. Click on the page or pasteboard to create a new frame at a default size. Drag to adjust the frame's dimensions.

To delete a frame:

- Select the frame object and press the **Delete** key. (If there's a selection point in the text, pressing **Delete** will remove characters after the cursor.)

Putting text into a frame

You can put text into a frame in one of five ways:

1 WritePlus story editor:

- Right-click on a frame and choose **Edit Story** (shortcut **Ctrl+E** with text selected) to start **WritePlus**, PagePlus's integrated story editor.

2 Importing text:

- Right-click on a frame and choose **Text File...** (shortcut **Ctrl+T**) to import text.

3 Typing into the frame:

- Select the Pointer tool, then click for an insertion point to type text straight into a frame, or edit existing text. (See **Editing text on the page** on p. 83.)

4 Pasting via the Clipboard:

- Select the Pointer tool and click for an insertion point in the text, then press **Ctrl+V**.

> TIP: Using the **Edit/Paste Special...** command gives you a choice of formatting options.

5 Drag and drop:

- Select text (e.g. in a word processor file), then drag it onto your page.

If you drop onto a selected a frame, the text is pasted inline after existing text. Otherwise, a new frame is created for the text.

Frame setup and layout

The **frame layout** controls how text will flow in the frame. The frame can contain multiple **columns**. When a frame is selected (and the Frames option is switched on in the View menu), its column margins appear as dashed grey guide lines. Note that unlike the **page margin and row/column guides**, which serve as layout guides for placing page elements, the frame column guides actually determine how text flows within each frame. Text won't flow outside the column guides.

You can drag the column guides or use a dialog to adjust the top and bottom **column blinds** and the left and right **column margins**.

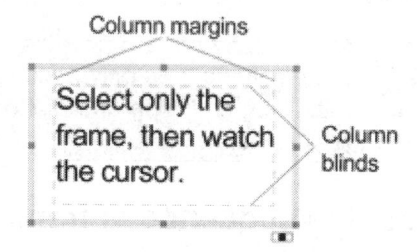

To edit frame properties directly:

- Select the frame object, then drag column guide lines to adjust the boundaries of the column.

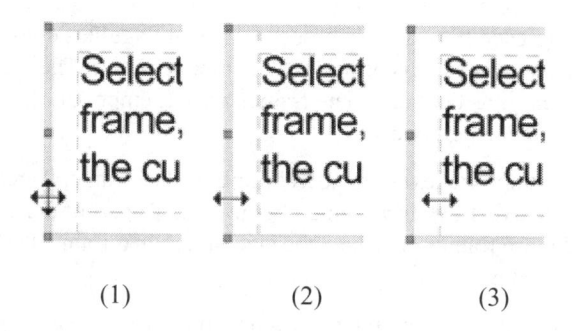

(1)   (2)   (3)

The illustration above shows how the cursor changes to show when you're (1) over the frame's bounding box or (2) over one of its column boundaries.

In (3), the left frame margin has been dragged in slightly. Notice how paragraph indents are preserved relative to the margin guide.

Note that the frame's handles use the colour you've assigned to the **layer** it's on.

To edit frame properties using a dialog:

1. Select the frame and click the ![icon] **Frame Setup** button on the Frame context bar.
2. To change the number of columns, gutter (gap), or left/right frame margins, enter values in the appropriate boxes in the Frame Setup dialog.
3. To change the column blinds (top and bottom frame margins), click a cell in the table and enter a new value.

> **TIP:** If the frame has more than one column, you only need to enter top/bottom values for the first one. Then click **Top** and/or **Bottom** to repeat the entries instantly in the cells below.

How a story flows through a sequence of frames

You can have just one frame on its own, or you can have many frames. Frames can be connected in linked **sequences**.

The **story** associated with a given frame sequence flows through the first frame on to the next and keeps flowing into frames in the link sequence.

A key difference from a word processor is that PagePlus does not normally add or remove frames according to the amount of text. The text simply flows until the text runs out (and some frames are left empty), or the frames run out (and some text is left over).

If there is still more text to go after filling the last frame, PagePlus stores it in an invisible **overflow area**, remembering that it's part of the story text. If you later add more frames or reduce the size of text in a frame, the rest of the story text is flowed in.

If the text runs out before the last frame, you have some empty frames. These frames will be filled with text if you add more text to the story, or if you increase the size of the story text.

You can use the **AutoFit** function or the frame's **AutoFlow** button to scale a story's text size so it fits exactly into the available frames. See **Fitting text to frames** on p. 93.

PagePlus keeps track of multiple linked frame sequences, and lets you flow several stories in the same publication. The **Text Manager** (accessed via the Tools menu) provides an overview of all stories and lets you choose which one you want to edit.

Linking frames

When selected, a text frame includes a **Link** button at the bottom right which allows you to import text files or control how the frame's story flows to following frames. The icon inside each frame's Link button denotes the state of the frame and its story text:

No Overflow
The frame is not linked to a following frame (it's either a standalone frame or the last frame in a sequence) and the end of the story text is visible.

Overflow
The frame is not linked (either standalone or last frame) and there is additional story text in the overflow area. An **AutoFlow** button also appears to the left of the Link button.

Continued
The frame is linked to a following frame. The end of the story text may be visible, or it may flow into the following frame.

> NOTE: The button icon will be red if the final frame of the sequence is overflowing, or green if there's no overflow.

There are two basic ways to set up a linked sequence of frames:

- You can link a sequence of empty frames, then import the text.
  OR
  You can import the text into a single frame, then create and link additional frames into which the text automatically flows.

> NOTE: When frames are created by the **AutoFlow** option (for example when importing text), they are automatically linked in sequence.

To link the selected frame to another frame as the next frame:

- Click the frame's [+] **Link** button.
  OR
  Select the frame, then click the [icon] **Link Frame** button on the Frame context bar.

- Click with the Textflow cursor on the frame to be linked to. Only empty frames are valid frames to link to.

To unlink the selected frame from the sequence:

- Click the [icon] **Unlink Frame** button on the Frame context bar.
  OR
  Click on the frame's **Link** button, then click with the Textflow cursor on the same frame.

Story text remains with the "old" frames. For example, if you detach the second frame of a three-frame sequence, the story text remains in the first and third frames, which are now linked into a two-frame story. The detached frame is always empty.

To navigate from frame to frame:

- Click the [icon] **Previous Frame** or [icon] **Next Frame** button on the Frame context bar.

Graphic properties of frames

Like graphics, frames have **line, fill, and transparency** properties—initially an outline of zero weight, a clear fill, and transparency set to None. As with graphics, you can edit these properties, for example adding a grey or light-coloured fill as shading behind a frame's text. You can also import images **inline** with frame text, and wrap text around any type of frame.

Using artistic text

Artistic text is standalone text you type directly onto a page. Especially useful for headlines, pull quotes, and other special-purpose text, it's easily formatted with the standard text tools but has some artistic advantages over frame text. For example, you can initially "draw" artistic text at a desired point size, and drag it to adjust the size later. Unlike the characters in a text frame, an artistic text object can take different line styles, fills (including gradient and Bitmap fills), and transparency for stunning pictorial effects. You can flip artistic text and it will remain editable. And artistic text can even be made to flow along a **curved path** for uniquely creative typographic effects!

artistic

To create artistic text:

1. Choose the **Artistic Text Tool** from the Artistic Text flyout on the Tools toolbar.
2. Click anywhere on the page for an insertion point using a default point size, or drag to specify a particular size as shown here.
3. Set initial text properties (font, style, etc.) as needed before typing, using the Text context bar, Format menu, or right-click (and choose **Text Format>**).

   Type normally to enter text.

Once you've created an artistic text object, you can select, move, resize, delete, and copy it just as you would with a text frame.

To resize or reproportion an artistic text object:

- Drag the object's handles to resize it while maintaining the object's proportions. To resize freely, hold down the **Shift** key while dragging.

To edit artistic text:

- Select a range of text by dragging. Double-click to select a word, or triple-click to select a paragraph.

Now you can type new text, apply character and paragraph formatting, edit the text in WritePlus, apply proofing options, and so on.

Putting text on a path

"Ordinary" straight-line **artistic text** is far from ordinary—but you can extend its creative possibilities even further by flowing it along a curved path. The resulting object has all the properties of artistic text, plus its path is a Bézier curve that you can edit with the Pointer tool as easily as any other line! In addition, text on a path is editable in some unique ways, as described below.

PagePlus offers four ways to create text on a path, i.e.

To apply a preset curved path to text:

1. Create an artistic text object.
2. With the text selected, click the **Path flyout** on the Text context bar and choose a preset path.

The text now flows along the specified path.

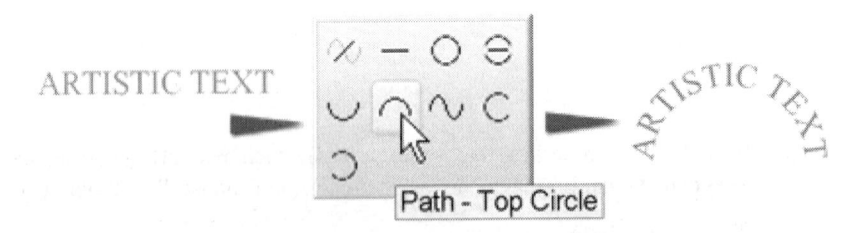

To add artistic text along an existing line or shape:

1. Create a freehand, straight, or curved line (see **Drawing and editing lines** on p. 139) or a shape (see **Drawing and editing shapes** on p. 145).
2. Choose the **A** **Artistic Text Tool** from the Artistic Text flyout on the Tools toolbar.
3. Bring the cursor very close to the line. When the cursor changes to include a curve, click the mouse where you want the text to begin, and the line changes as shown below.

> NOTE: If you don't want text on a path, you can override the cursor response by holding down the **Alt** key.

4. Begin typing at the insertion point. Text flows along the line, which has been converted to a path.

To fit existing text to an existing line or shape:
1. Create an artistic text object.
2. Create a freehand, straight, or curved line.
3. Select both objects and choose **Fit Text to Curve** from the Tools menu. The text now flows along the specified path.

> NOTE: The original line object no longer exists. To recover it, use **Undo** at this point.

To create text and path at the same time:
1. Choose one of the Path Text tools from the Artistic Text flyout:

   The **Freehand Path Text** tool lets you sketch a curved line in a freeform way

   The **Straight Path Text** tool is for drawing a straight line

   The **Curved Path Text** tool lets you join a series of line segments (which may be curved or straight) using "connect the dots" mouse clicks.

2. Create a line on the page (press **Esc** or double-click to end a Curved Path). Your line appears as a path with an insertion point at its starting end.
3. Begin typing at the insertion point, and text flows along the path.

Editing text on a path

Artistic text on a path remains editable as text. Likewise, you can continue to edit its path with the Pointer tool and Curve context bar, as described in **Drawing and editing lines**.

When a path text object is selected, you'll notice that text paths have several unique "handles" not found on other objects. You may need to zoom in a bit, but it's easy to select the handles—special cursors let you know when you're directly over them. To see what the handles do, carefully compare these two examples:

Baseline Shift Handle   Start / End Handles

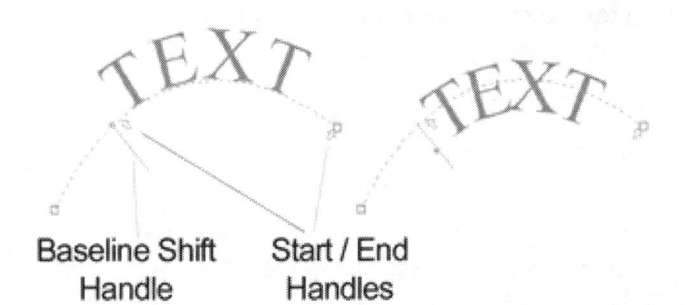

- The **Baseline Shift** handle, indicated by a cursor, resembles a QuickShape handle with a tiny slider control. Drag the slider to raise and lower the text with respect to the path. In the right-hand example above, we've lowered the original text.

- The **Start** and **End** handles, indicated by START and END cursors, look like arrows. Drag them to adjust where the text begins and ends with respect to the path's start and end nodes. In the above example, we've shifted the text to the left by dragging the Start handle.

You can flip text from one side of a path to the other by reversing curves. This switches the start and end nodes of the path, so the text runs in the other direction. It's handy, for example, if you want to move text from the outside to the inside of a circular path, to run counter-clockwise rather than clockwise, or vice versa. Note that the text isn't mirrored—it still reads correctly!

To reverse the text path:

- Select the path text object and click the **Reverse Curves** button on the Curve context bar.

Whichever method you used to create a path text object, you can always detach the text as a separate artistic text object by removing its path.

To remove the text path:
1. Select the path text object.
2. Click the [icon] **Path-None** button on the Text context bar's Path flyout.

The text remains as a straight-line artistic text object; the path is permanently removed.

Editing text on the page

You can use the Pointer tool to edit **frame text, table text,** or **artistic text** directly. On the page, you can select and enter text, set paragraph indents and tab stops, change text properties, apply text styles, and use **Find and Replace**. For editing longer stories, and for more advanced options, choose WritePlus.

Selecting and entering text

To edit text on the page:
- Select the Pointer tool, then click or drag in the text object. A standard insertion point appears at the click position, or a range of text is selected, ready for the text to be edited.

> **TIP:** You can double-click to select a word, or triple-click to select a paragraph.

Sharon and the rabbit kept walking. |It was very peaceful, and the sun was setting gracefully behind the shock of trees at the far end of the grounds.

Sharon and the rabbit kept walking. It was very peaceful, and the sun was setting gracefully behind the shock of trees at the far end of the grounds.

To start a new paragraph:
- Press **Enter**.

To start a new line within the same paragraph (using a "line break" or "soft return"):
- Press Shift+Enter.

The following three options apply only to frame text. You can use these shortcuts or choose the items from the **Insert/Break** submenu.

To flow text to the next column (Column Break), frame (Frame Break) or page (Page Break):

- Press Ctrl+Enter, Alt+Enter or Ctrl+Shift+Enter, respectively.

To switch between insert mode and overwrite mode:

- Press the **Insert** key.

To repeat a text action:

- Choose **Repeat** from the Edit menu, or press **Ctrl+Y**.

For example, if you've applied new formatting to one paragraph, you can click in another paragraph and use the **Repeat** command to apply the same formatting there.

Setting paragraph indents

When a text object is selected, markers on the horizontal ruler indicate the left indent, first line indent, and right indent of the current paragraph. You can adjust the markers to set paragraph indents, or use a dialog.

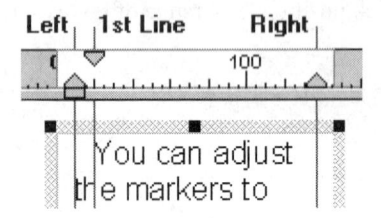

- The **Left** indent is set in relation to the object's left margin.
- The **1st line** indent is in relation to the left indent.
- The **Right** indent is in relation to the object's right margin.

For details on setting frame margins, see **Frame setup and layout** on p. 75.

To set the indents of the current paragraph:

- Drag the appropriate ruler marker(s).
  OR
  To adjust indent settings numerically, choose **Paragraph...** from the Format menu (or **Text Format/Paragraph...** from the right-click menu). You can enter values for Left, Right or Special (1st Line or Hanging) indents in the Indentation section.

Setting tab stops

To set a tab stop:
1. Select the paragraph(s) in which you want to set tab stops.
2. Click the ruler intersection button until it changes to the type of tab you want: (Left, Centre, Right, or Decimal).

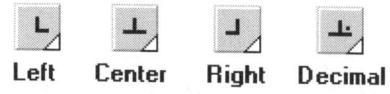

    Left   Center   Right   Decimal

3. Click on the horizontal ruler where you want to set a tab stop.

- To move a tab stop, drag it to a new ruler position.
- To delete a tab stop, drag it off the ruler.

> NOTE: If you want to set precise measurements for tabs, right-click the frame and choose **Text Format**, then select **Tabs...** from the submenu.

Working with Unicode text

PagePlus fully supports Unicode, making it possible to incorporate foreign characters or special symbols.

- To paste Unicode text from the Clipboard to the page, use **Edit/Paste Special....**

- Insert Unicode characters directly into your text by typing your Unicode Hex value and pressing Alt-X. The Alt-X keyboard operation toggles between the displayed character (e.g., @) and its Hex value (e.g., U+0040) equivalent.

- To export text in Unicode format, use WritePlus.

Editing story text with WritePlus

WritePlus is the story editor built into PagePlus. For certain tasks, such as viewing and editing the full text of an entire story that may be spread over many frames or pages, it's much more convenient than **Editing text on the page**. And for other tasks, such as exporting story text or **Marking index entries**, it's essential!

> NOTE: You can also use WritePlus to edit artistic text, but not table text.

To launch WritePlus:

- Right-click on a text frame or artistic text object and choose **Edit Story** (or with text selected, press **Ctrl+E** or choose **Edit Story** from the Edit menu). WritePlus opens with the object's story text.

The WritePlus environment

WritePlus opens in a separate window that shares many of the standard PagePlus menus and toolbars. As you make changes in WritePlus, story text in the main window updates instantly.

The WritePlus workspace can have one or two windows. Initially, you'll see the **Text Entry window**.

To display a **Style pane** on the left, click the ![icon] **Style Pane** button.

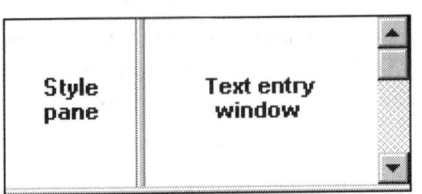

Style pane	Text entry window

WritePlus opens in **Layout Mode**, displaying text with formatting applied. You can quickly switch to **Draft Mode**, which doesn't display formatting variations.

To switch between Draft Mode and Layout Mode:

- Click the ![icon] **Formatting** button on the Story toolbar.

![icon] The Story toolbar, unique to WritePlus, includes other tools to assist you in working with story text. For example, the **Story list** lets you select the story

to be edited, or change the name of a story by typing in the list. Click the **Word Count** button to run a wizard that counts total words or characters, or the number of occurrences of a specified word.

To close WritePlus and return to PagePlus:

- Click the ✓ **Finish** button or the window's ☒ **Close** button.

Using Find and Replace

You can search publication text for an extraordinary variety of items: not just words or parts of words, but a host of character and paragraph attributes such as fonts, styles, alignment, bullets and numbering, missing fonts, drop caps... ... even inline graphics and more! Using the Find and Replace dialog—which remains open without interrupting your work until you click its **Close** button—you can replace globally, or on a case-by-case basis.

To use Find and Replace:

1. Choose **Find & Replace...** from the Edit menu or press **Ctrl+F**.

2. In the dialog, type the text to be found in the **Find** box and its replacement text (if any) in the **Replace** box. Click the down arrows to view recent items. Click either box's button to use flyout menus to select formats or special characters, or define a regular expression (for a wildcard-type search).

3. Select the Range to be searched: **Current Story** (just the currently selected text object or story), or **All Stories** (all text), or **Current Selection** (only used with the Replace All function to operate on the currently selected text).

4. Select **Match whole word only** to match character sequences that have **white space** (space, tab character, page break etc.) or punctuation at each end, or which are at the start/end of a paragraph. Select **Match case** for case-sensitive search. Select **Regular expressions** to treat the contents of the Find box as an expression, rather than as a literal string to be found.

5. Click **Find Next** to locate the next instance of the Find text. Then click **Replace** if you want to substitute the replacement text. Click **Find Next** again to continue searching.
   OR
   Click **Replace All** to replace all instances of the Find text with the replacement text. PagePlus reports when the search is completed.

6. Click **Close** to dismiss the Find and Replace dialog.

The Find and Replace dialog also lets you perform a wildcard-type search by using a **regular expression**—a formula for generating a set of strings—to specify complex search criteria. This is covered in more detail in PagePlus Help.

Inserting footnotes and endnotes

Within **frame text**, it's easy to add **footnotes** (which normally go at the bottom of a column) and/or **endnotes** (normally at the end of a text story). In either case you can customise the consecutive numbering or symbols used by reference marks, the style of both marks and note body text, and the placement and layout of note text, including optional line separators. You can add and view notes either on the page or in WritePlus.

To insert a footnote or endnote:

1. Click for an insertion point in a text frame. If updating an existing custom mark, select it first. (To view notes in WritePlus, check **Note Pane** on the View menu.) You cannot insert notes in artistic text.

2. Choose **Footnote/Endnote...** from the Insert menu.

3. Select either the **Footnote** or **Endnote** tab.

4. Set the Number format, Start at, Restart each and Note position fields as appropriate.

PagePlus displays the new footnote/endnote followed by a text edit cursor, so you can immediately enter the text of the note.

Formatting

Setting text properties

PagePlus gives you a high degree of typographic control over characters and paragraphs, whether you're working with **frame text**, **table text**, or **artistic text**.

To apply basic text formatting:

1. Select the text.

2. Use buttons on the Text context bar to change font, point size, font style, and paragraph alignment.

> NOTE: If a font is unavailable and has been substituted, its font name on the Context Bar is prefixed by the "?" character.

Default text properties

Default text properties are the settings used for text you type into any new text object. You can change these settings directly from selected text, or using the Text Style Palette. The Palette has the advantage of letting you review all the settings at a glance.

To change default text properties:

1. Create a single sample of text and fine-tune its properties as desired—or use existing text that already has the right properties.
2. Select the text or container and choose **Update Object Default** from the Format menu.

PagePlus will preserve the formatting of imported word-processor text. If you've imported or pasted some text and want to apply different formatting, you can first reset the text to use the default text properties.

To clear custom formatting (restore plain/default text properties):

- Select a range of text and choose **Clear Text Formatting** from the Format menu.
  OR
  Click the down arrow on the Styles box and select **Clear Formatting** in the drop-down list.

The PagePlus Help provides a Text Properties summary for detailed reference.

Using text styles

It's a good idea to establish the main text and graphic formatting to be used in your publication early in the creative process. PagePlus facilitates this by letting you define named **text styles**, which can be applied to **frame text**, **table text**, or **artistic text**. A text style is a set of character and/or paragraph attributes saved as a group. When you apply a style to text, you apply the whole group of attributes in just one step. For example, you could define named paragraph styles for particular layout elements, such as "Heading," "Sidebar," or "Body Text," and character styles to convey meaning, such as "Emphasis," "Price," or "Date Reference." Using styles not only speeds the task of laying out a publication but ensures consistency and ease of updating.

Paragraph styles and character styles

A **paragraph style** is a complete specification for the appearance of a paragraph, including all its font and paragraph format attributes.

> NOTE: Every paragraph in PagePlus has a paragraph style associated with it.

- PagePlus includes one built-in paragraph style called **"Normal,"** with a specification consisting of generic attributes including left-aligned, 12pt Times New Roman. Initially, the "Normal" style is the default for any new paragraph text you type. You can modify the "Normal" style by redefining any of its attributes, and create any number of new styles having different names and attributes.

- Applying a paragraph style to text updates all the text in the paragraph except sections that have been locally formatted. For example, a single word marked as bold would remain bold when the paragraph style was updated.

A **character style** includes only font attributes (such as font name, point size, bold, italic, etc.), and you apply it at the character level—that is, to a range of selected characters—rather than to the whole paragraph.

- Typically, a character style applies emphasis (such as italics, bolding or colour) to whatever underlying font the paragraph already uses; the assumption is that you want to keep that underlying font the same. The base character style is shown in the Text Style Palette simply as "Default Paragraph Font," which has no specified attributes but basically means "whatever font the paragraph style already uses."

- The Default Paragraph Font appears in the Styles box as **"Clear Formatting"** because applying it strips any local formatting you've added and restores the original text attributes for the paragraph. (In fact it has the same effect as the **Clear Text Formatting** command on the Format menu.)

- As with paragraph styles, you can define any number of new character styles using different names and attributes. Custom character styles don't usually include a specific font name or point size, but there's no rule against including them.

Working with named styles

[Body Text ▼] The named style of the currently selected text appears in the drop-down **Styles** box on the Text context bar. The box may show a character style (if one is applied locally); otherwise it indicates the paragraph style. You can use either the Styles box or a dialog to apply a particular style to existing text, modify an existing style, or define a new style.

To apply a named style:
1. Using the Pointer tool, click in a paragraph (if applying a paragraph style) or select a range of text (if applying a character style).
2. Click the down arrow on the Styles box and select the style name in the drop-down list.

To update a named style using the properties of existing text:
1. Make any desired changes to some text that uses the named style as shown in the Styles box.
2. Click the arrow on the Styles box and select the current style name again from the list. Click **OK** to confirm the option to "Update the style to reflect recent changes."

All text using the named style, throughout the publication, takes on the new properties.

To define a new style using the properties of existing text:
1. Format the text as desired.
2. To define a character style, select a range of reformatted text. To define a paragraph style, deselect text but leave a blinking cursor (insertion point) within the newly formatted section.
3. Type a new style name into the Styles box and press **Enter**.

The new style is defined with the properties of the selected text.

To modify an existing style or define a new one using a dialog:
1. Choose **Text Style Palette...** from the Format menu.
2. To modify an existing style, select the style name and click **Modify...**.
3. Use the **Style Properties** dialog to define (or change) the style name, base style, and following style. Click the **Attributes** button to access dialogs that let you specify any text attributes you want to include in the style definition.
4. Click **OK** to accept style properties, or **Cancel** to abandon changes.

5. Click **Apply** to update text, or click **Close** to maintain the style in the publication for future use.

To import one or more styles from another PagePlus file:
1. Choose **Text Style Palette...** from the Format menu.
2. Click the **Import...** button and use the dialog to locate the file from which styles should be imported, and the specific style(s) to be imported.

Importing styles

When you use the **Insert/Text File...** command to import text from a word-processor file, you can choose whether or not to retain the source file's named styles.

- Check **Retain Format** in the Import Text dialog if you want PagePlus to import and retain these styles. Any text not tagged with a style will be marked with the "Normal" style as used in your publication.

- Uncheck **Retain Format** to discard styles; PagePlus will mark all text with the "Normal" style, as for unstyled text in the case above.

Adjusting letter spacing and kerning

Letter spacing (tracking)

The spacing between characters in a paragraph can have a subtle effect on the reader. PagePlus lets you experiment with the letter spacing of text. The normal value is expressed as 0%. Increase the value to spread text apart, and reduce it to tighten letter spacing.

To adjust letter spacing between characters:
1. Select a range of text with the Pointer tool.
2. Display the Character tab and choose a value from the AV **Letter spacing** drop-down list box, or type in a new value.

Kerning

Kerning is normally applied where two large, adjacent characters look over- or under-spaced due to the shape of the characters, and is used to reduce or increase the space between the pair of characters.

AV For example, the letters 'A' and 'V' look over-spaced when placed adjacent to each other.

AV Kerning solves this problem by bringing the two letters closer together.

To adjust kerning between a letter pair:
1. Using the Pointer tool, click between the two characters for an insertion point.
2. To increase space (positive kerning), press **Ctrl+Alt+'+'**.
   To decrease space (negative kerning), press **Ctrl+Alt+'-'**.

Typically the advantages of kerning are only noticeable on larger text, so the most detailed attention is applied to kerning when creating display text: headlines or text logos. As a rule of thumb, you should apply pair-kerning to text over 16 points. You can turn auto pair-kerning on or off, and change the point size above which it is applied.

Fitting text to frames

Fitting story text precisely into a sequence of frames is part of the art of laying out publications.

If there's too much story text to fit in a frame sequence, PagePlus stores it in an invisible **overflow area** and the Link button on the last frame of the sequence displays [+] and an **AutoFlow** button appears next to the Link button. You might edit the story down or make more room for it by adding an extra frame or two to the sequence. Clicking the AutoFlow button adds additional frames and pages as needed (see below).

The Frame context bar includes several tools that can simplify the task of fitting text to frames:

AutoFit
Click to scale the story's text size so it fits exactly into the available frames. You can use this early on, to gauge how the story fits, or near the end, to apply the finishing touch. AutoFit first applies small point size changes, then small leading changes, then adjustments to the paragraph space below value, until the text fits. Other settings are not affected. (Also see Note below.)

> **TIP:** You can also press **Ctrl+Alt+X** to apply AutoFit.

Enlarge Story Text
Click to increase the story's text size one increment. Double-click for a bigger increase.

Shrink Story Text
Click to reduce the story's text size one increment. Double-click for a greater reduction.

AutoFlow

When importing text, it's a good idea to take advantage of the **AutoFlow** feature, which will automatically create text frames and pages until all the text has been imported. This way, enough frames are created to display the whole story. Then you can gauge just how much adjustment will be needed to fit the story to the available "real estate" in your publication.

If you add more text to a story while editing, or have reduced the size of frame, you may find that an overflow condition crops up. In this case (see above) you can decide whether to use AutoFit or click the frame's **AutoFlow** button.

To AutoFlow story text on the page:

- Click the AutoFlow button just to the left of the frame's **Link** button.

Wrapping text to an object

PagePlus lets you wrap frame text around the contours of a separate object. Usually, this means wrapping text to a picture that overlaps or sits above a text frame. But you can wrap frame text around an artistic text object, a table or another frame, or even flow text inside a graphic (a circle, for example). Wrapping is accomplished by changing the **wrap setting** for the object to which text will wrap.

Wrap options are accessible via the **Wrap Settings** dialog, which includes these useful illustrations of how text flows in each instance:

| None | Top & bottom | Square | Tight | Inside | Edge |

To wrap text around an object:

- Click the ⊞ **Wrap Settings** button on the Arrange toolbar, or choose **Wrap Settings...** from the Arrange menu.

The Wrap Settings dialog lets you select the manner in which text will wrap around the sides of the object. With **Tight** wrapping, text wraps closely around the object's contours.

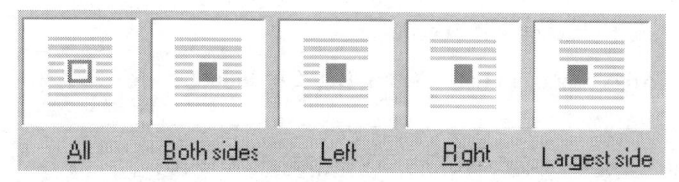

| All | Both sides | Left | Right | Largest side |

In addition, you can specify the **Distance from text**: the "standoff" between the object's **wrap outline** and adjacent text. The wrap outline is a contour that defines the object's edges for text wrapping purposes. Different object types have different initial wrap outlines. For QuickShapes the wrap outline corresponds exactly to the object's edges, while for closed shapes the outline is a rectangle to start with.

You can manually adjust the wrap outline using the Curve context bar for more precise text fitting. See the PagePlus Help for more information.

Flowing text around inline images

An "inline" image is one you've **imported** when there's an insert point in a text object, or have pasted into a text object. (And where text flow is concerned, inline **picture frames** behave just like inline images.) Both **frame** and **artistic** text will flow around an inline image if the picture's alignment setting is Left, Centre, Right, or Indent, but not if it's Top, Middle, or Bottom. You can also adjust the Distance from text, which (as with regular text wrap) affects the "standoff" between the object and adjacent text. In the illustration at right below, the standoff is .5 cm all round.

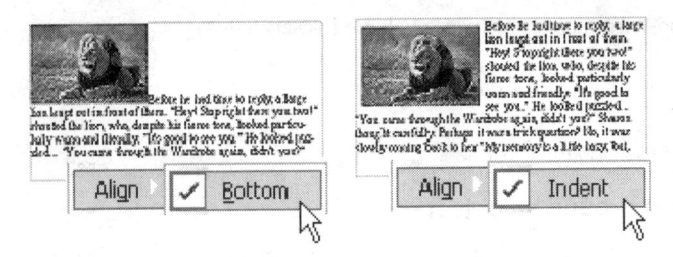

With frame text, the effect is similar to wrapping around a separate object, as detailed above. Lines of artistic text, on the other hand, are only terminated by line breaks and don't wrap—rather they break around the image and the text object expands to the right.

To flow text around an inline image or picture frame:

1. Right-click it and choose **Properties....**

2. Set the "Align" option to **Left**, **Centre**, **Right**, or **Indent**.

> NOTE: You can also right-click an inline image and choose **Align**, then select an option from the submenu.

3. In the Picture Properties dialog, set the indent amount (if any) and the **Distance from text**, then click **OK**. You can also adjust the indent amount by dragging the picture left or right.

Creating a bulleted or numbered list

You can turn a paragraph into a bulleted or numbered list. Each time you insert a following return, the new line will begin with the specified symbol. Typing two returns in a row (pressing **Enter** twice) cancels bullets or numbers and resumes regular paragraph formatting.

To create a bulleted or numbered list:

1. Right-click the paragraph and choose **Text Format>Bullets & Numbering....**

2. Click either the **Bulleted** tab or the **Numbered** tab.

3. To choose from preset formats, click the **Presets** button.
OR
Select custom settings for the list (click the **Details** button to redisplay custom options from the Presets pane).
- For bullets, you can set the **Bullet indent** and **Text indent** distances, and pick a bullet character either from the top row or the **Bullet** list. Click the **Font...** button to define other attributes, including colour.
- For numbers, you can select a numbering **Format**, an optional **Separator** character, and set the **Number indent** and **Text indent** distances. Click the **Font...** button to define other attributes, including colour. Uncheck **Restart Numbering** to continue the numbering sequence from the previous list in the same story; otherwise, check the option and select a specific **Start at** value.

4. Click **OK** to apply list formatting.

To turn off bullets or numbering for a selected paragraph:

- In the **Bullets & Numbering...** dialog, click the **None** preset option on either the **Bulleted** tab or the **Numbered** tab.

Creating ruled lines

You can use ruled lines to set a block of text apart from its surroundings. For example, you might employ ruled lines above and below a "pull quote" inserted alongside a newsletter article.

> **NOTE:** You can also use the Border Edges tab of the Line and Border dialog to **apply edges selectively** to an object.

To create a ruled line:

1. Right-click the paragraph and choose **Text Format>Paragraph...**.
2. Click the **Line** tab.
3. In the Line Selection box, click one of the upper squares to select a line above, or one of the lower squares for a line below. Clicking the middle square selects both.
4. To customise the line style, select one or both of the line previews (**Shift**-click to toggle), then click the **Line Style...** button.
5. In the Line dialog, choose line properties including weight, style, colour, and corners. To restore no lines above/below, click **None**. Click **OK** when you're done.

6. Back on the **Line** tab, specify left/right indent and gap settings for the line(s). The Preview window shows the effect applied to a sample paragraph.

7. Click **OK** to apply the effect to the selected paragraph.

Using Special Characters

You can insert any character from any font installed on your system, using either the Insert menu or (for common symbols) keyboard shortcuts (see PagePlus Help). You can also use a convenient keyboard switch to enter **subscripts** or **superscripts**.

To insert a symbol character using the Insert menu:

1. Select the Pointer tool and click in the text for an insertion point.

2. Choose **Symbol...** from the Insert menu, and select a symbol from the submenu.

3. If you need a symbol not shown on the submenu, select **Other** to display the Insert Symbol dialog. The dialog remains open so you can continue editing in the workspace as you select symbols.

4. • Select a **Font** to display its full character set, and then scroll the font table to view characters. You can choose from the **Subset** list to jump to a particular range within the character set.
   • Click any individual character (or select it while browsing using the arrow keys on your keyboard) to view the character's name and Unicode Index at the bottom of the dialog. You can also enter any Unicode hex value and click Go to jump to that particular character in the current font.
   • To insert a character into your text, double-click it (or select it and click **Insert**).

To enter subscript or superscript characters:

- Press **Ctrl+=** to enter subscript mode, or **Ctrl+Shift+=** to for superscript mode. Type the subscript or superscript, then press the key combination again to return to entering regular characters.

Inserting date/time

You can insert a date/time field into your text, stamped with current date/time information. Various date and time formats are available. By default, the date/time field updates itself automatically. You can turn auto-updating off if necessary.

To insert a date/time field:

1. Select the Pointer tool and click in the text for an insertion point.
2. Choose **Information** from the Insert menu, then select **Date or Time...** from the submenu. Select a date/time format.
3. To keep the original date/time stamp in place indefinitely, uncheck **Update Automatically**.

To edit the information in a date/time field:

- Select the field and choose **Information/Date or Time...** from the Insert menu.

Inserting user details

When you create a publication using a Design Template for the first time, you will be prompted for user details (from a User Details dialog) which can then be used for subsequent design templates. This means you don't need to re-enter the same information the next time it's required in your next Design Template.

You can employ the User Details dialog to review all your User Details at a glance, and update fields directly at any time.

> TIP: User details will be prompted for every time you load a Design Template. To switch off, uncheck the **Show when opening new templates** check box in the User Details dialog.

To add, edit or change User Details:

1. Choose **Set User Details...** from the Tools menu.
2. Enter new information into the spaces on the **Home**, **Business**, or **Custom** tab.

You can also insert one or more User Detail field into any publication at any time. The **Custom** tab of the User Details dialog includes blank, renameable fields where you can enter any information you may frequently need to "plug into" your publications.

To insert a User Detail field:

1. Select the Pointer tool and click in the text for an insertion point.
2. Choose **Information** from the Insert menu, then select **User Details...** from the submenu. Select a User Detail entry.

Viewing and changing document information

PagePlus maintains basic properties and statistics for each publication file.

To view or change document properties:

1. Choose **Properties...** from the File menu.
2. Click the **Summary** tab to view or change fields for Title, Subject, Author, Keywords, and Comments.
3. Click the **Statistics** tab to view key dates, page count, etc.

To insert document information in your text:

1. Select the Pointer tool and click in the text for an insertion point.
2. Choose **Information** from the Insert menu, then select **Publication Info...** from the submenu. Select a property to insert and click **OK**.

If the document information changes, the document information field in the text is automatically updated.

Using hyphenation

Hyphenation is usually accomplished automatically in PagePlus using **auto-hyphenation**. This feature recognises and corrects lines which would otherwise be too ragged or use overly large word spacing. You can turn it off, if desired, or change the hyphenation settings.

The **hot zone** is the amount of extra space at the end of each line that is considered acceptable. If the amount of extra space exceeds this value, then auto-hyphenation will try to split words to reduce the excess.

The **minimum word size** is the minimum number of characters that a word must have before it is considered valid to hyphenate the word at the end of a line.

Letters before and **after** determine the minimum number of letters each part of a word must contain if the word is split by auto-hyphenation.

Hyphenation points (viewable in WritePlus only) can be inserted into specific words to override auto-hyphenation. Perhaps a word you are using breaks onto a new line at the wrong place—an inserted hyphenation point in the word will force the word to always break at that hyphenation point (the hyphen will display automatically). WritePlus displays the hyphenation point as a "¬" (NOT SIGN) character.

To access auto-hyphenation settings:
1. Choose **Paragraph...** from the Format menu and select the **Hyphenation** tab.
2. To turn off auto-hyphenation, uncheck **Auto Hyphenation**.
3. Use the controls to adjust auto-hyphenation settings for successive hyphens, hot zone, word size, and letters before/after.

To insert a hyphenation point:
1. Click in the story text where you want to mark a hyphenation point.
2. Select **Insert> Hyphenation Point**.

OR:

1. In WritePlus, switch on ¶ **Special characters**, and with the Pointer tool, click in the text where you want to mark a hyphenation point.
2. Choose **Hyphenation Point** from the Insert menu, to place the "¬"character.

To remove a hyphenation point in WritePlus:
- The hyphenation point can be removed by backspacing over the "¬" character (use the Backspace key). Ensure the **Special characters** button is switched on.

Checking and fixing hyphenation points is usually one of the "finishing touches" to a publication. For example, an auto-hyphenated text block using "justified" alignment may have some lines with large, ugly gaps between words. To fill a line out, you can insert a hyphenation point in a word a bit further on, so that the line breaks at a more attractive place.

A hyphenation point in a word overrides auto-hyphenation of the word. To ensure a word is never broken by auto-hyphenation (for instance, to reduce the number of hyphens in a narrow column of text), insert a hyphenation point before the first character of the word.

Hyphenation points work even if auto-hyphenation is turned off.

Using AutoCorrect and AutoSpell

PagePlus includes two powerful support tools to nip possible spelling errors in the bud. The **AutoCorrect** feature overcomes common typing errors and lets you build a custom list of letter combinations and substitutions (correction list) to be applied automatically as you type. You can also turn on **AutoSpell** feature to mark possible problem words in your story text in red. Both features apply to frame text, table text, and artistic text.

If you prefer to address spelling issues in larger doses, at any point along the way you can run the **Spell Checker**.

AutoCorrect

To set options for automatic text correction:

1. Choose **Options...** from the Tools menu and select the **Auto-Correct** page.

2. Check your desired correction options as required.
   - Correct two initial, consecutive capitals
   - Capitalise the first letter of sentences
   - Capitalise the names of days
   - Capitalise accidental usage of the Caps Lock key
   - Change straight quotes to typographic ("smart") quotes
   - Create a correction list (see below)

> NOTE: Check **Replace text while typing** to turn on AutoCorrect.

To create a correction list:

1. In the **Replace** field, type a name for the AutoCorrect entry. This is the abbreviation or word to be replaced automatically as you type. For example, if you frequently mistype "product" as "prodcut," type "prodcut" in the Replace box.

2. In the **With** field, type the text to be automatically inserted in place of the abbreviation or word in the **Replace** field.

3. Click the **Add** button to add the new entry to the list.

4. To modify an entry in the correction list, select it in the list, then edit it in the **Replace** and **With** field above. Click the **Replace** button.

5. To remove an entry, select it and click **Delete**.

To turn off AutoCorrect:

- Uncheck Replace text while typing.

AutoSpell

To turn AutoSpell on (or off):

1. Choose **Options...** from the Tools menu.

2. On the General tab, check (or uncheck) **Autospell**.

When AutoSpell is activated, possible problem words in your story text are marked in red, and you can view a list of suggested alternatives.

To view alternatives:

1. Right-click a marked word.
2. To replace a marked word, choose an alternative spelling from the menu.
3. To tell PagePlus to ignore (leave unmarked) all instances of the marked word in the publication, choose **Ignore All** from the right-click menu.
4. To add the marked word (as spelled) to your personal dictionary, choose **Add to Dictionary** from the right-click menu. This means PagePlus will ignore the word in any publication.
5. To run the Spell Checker, choose **Check Spelling...** from the menu.

Spell-checking

The **Spell Checker** lets you check the spelling of a single word, selected text, a single story, or all text in your publication. (To help trap spelling errors as they occur, use the PagePlus **AutoCorrect** and **AutoSpell** features.) You can customise the built-in dictionary by adding your own words.

Multilingual spell checking is supported by use of up to nine dictionaries. The US and UK dictionaries are supplied by default, with the remainder available on the *PagePlus 11 Resource CD*. Any language (if installed) can be enabled globally from **Tools>Options>General tab** or applied specifically to text or paragraphs via the Language Selector in the Character tab.

To check spelling:

1. (Optional) To check a single story, first make sure the text or text object is selected.
2. Choose **Spell Checker...** from the Tools menu.
   OR
   (In WritePlus) Click the ![abc] **Spell Check** button.
3. In the dialog, click **Options...** to set preferences for ignoring words in certain categories, such as words containing numbers or domain names.
4. Select **Check currently selected story only** or **Check all stories in my publication** to select the scope of the search.
5. Click **Start** to begin the spelling check.

When a problem is found, PagePlus highlights the problem word. The dialog offers alternative suggestions, and you can choose to **Change** or **Ignore** this instance (or all instances) of the problem word, with the option of adding the problem word to your dictionary. (See below for more on modifying your dictionary.)

6. Spell checking continues until you click the **Close** button or the spell-check is completed.

To check the spelling of a single word:

1. With the AutoSpell feature turned on, select in a marked word, then right-click. You'll see alternative spellings on the context menu.
2. To replace the word, choose an alternative spelling from the menu.
3. To tell PagePlus to ignore (leave unmarked) all instances of the marked word in the publication, choose **Ignore All**.
4. To add the marked word (as spelled) to your personal dictionary, choose **Add to Dictionary**. This means PagePlus will subsequently ignore the word in any publication.
5. To run the Spell Checker, choose **Check Spelling...**.

Modifying your dictionary

The Spell Checker relies on a built-in dictionary that's quite extensive but may not contain certain words you use frequently in your publications. To make spell-checking more efficient, you can add words to your own User Dictionary as described below so they won't pop up as "misspelled" in the future, and (if necessary) delete new words you previously added—especially handy if you misspelled one when you typed it in!

> NOTE: The User dictionary is designed to store words in any language.

To add or delete a word in the User Dictionary:

1. Choose **Options...** from the Tools menu and select the **Dictionary** page. The contents of the dictionary appear in an alphabetical list.
2. To add a word, type it into the box and click **Add**.
3. To delete a word, select it in the list and click **Delete**.

> NOTE: When selecting words, you can press **Ctrl** to select multiple words, or **Shift** to select a contiguous range.

You may wish to transfer your custom dictionary to another computer, use it with a new version of PagePlus, or pass it along for a friend or colleague to use.

To access your personal User Dictionary file:

- In Windows, search for the file named SsceUser.tlx. Normally this will be located in the PagePlus "Languages" folder.

Automatic proofreading

The **Proof Reader** checks for grammar and readability errors in selected text, a single story, or all text in your publication. You can use Proof Reader from either PagePlus or WritePlus.

To start the Proof Reader:

1. To check a single story, first make sure the text or text object is selected.
2. Choose **Proof Reader...** from the Tools menu.
3. If necessary, click the **Options** button to set options for proofreading, including a spell-check option and the level of formality (with checks for rule types).
4. Select **Check currently selected story only** or **Check all stories in my publication** to select the scope of the search.
5. Click **Start** to begin proof reading.

When a problem is found, PagePlus highlights the problem word. The dialog offers alternative suggestions, and you can choose to **Change** or **Ignore** this instance (or all instances) of the problem word.

6. Proofreading continues until you click the **Close** button or the process is completed.

Using the thesaurus

The **Thesaurus** lets you find synonyms, definitions, and variations of words in text objects throughout the publication. You can use the Thesaurus from either PagePlus or WritePlus.

To display the Thesaurus:

1. To look up a specific word, first drag to highlight it.
2. Choose **Thesaurus...** from the Tools menu or press **Shift+F7**.
3. To look up a different word, type it into the "Replace/Look Up" box and click the **Look Up** button.

Using the Thesaurus

If the word entered is found in the thesaurus database:

- The "Meanings" list shows definitions for the word in the "Looked Up" box. Initially, the first definition is selected.

- The "Synonyms" list shows synonyms for the definition selected in the "Meanings" box. Initially, the first synonym appears in the "Replace/Look Up" box.

To pop a new word into the "Replace/Look Up" box:

- Click the word in the "Synonyms" list.
  OR
  Type a new word directly into the "Replace/Look Up" box.

You can navigate indefinitely through the thesaurus by selecting the specific meaning, followed by the specific synonym you are interested in and then clicking on the **Look Up** button to get a new range of meanings and synonyms for the new word.

To replace the original word:

- Click the **Replace** button to replace the original word (selected in your text) with the word in the "Replace/Look Up" box.

To exit the thesaurus:

- Click the **Cancel** button.

Previewing the printed page

The **Print Preview** mode changes the screen view to display your layout without frames, guides, rulers, and other screen items. Special options, such as tiled output or crop marks, are not displayed.

To preview the printed page:

- Click the **Print Preview** button on the Standard toolbar.

In Print Preview mode, the lower toolbar provides a variety of familiar view options, plus the **Multipage View** button, which lets you preview your publication using a page array.

To arrange multiple pages in the preview window:

1. Click the ▦ **Multipage View** button. An array selector appears.
2. Click and drag to choose an array within the selector, e.g. 3x2 Pages. To expand the number of choices, drag up and to the right.

To return to single page view:

- Click the ▦ **Multipage** button and select the "1x1 page" array.

To cancel Print Preview mode:

- Click the **Close** button.

Working with Tables

Creating text-based tables

Tables are ideal for presenting text and data in a variety of easily customisable row-and-column formats, with built-in spreadsheet capabilities.

Quantity	Description	Code
12	Geraniums	34W-6YY
3	Plant Posts (small)	44X-123

Each cell in a table behaves like a mini-frame. There are many similarities (and several key differences) between **frame text** and table text.

- With table text, you can vary **character and paragraph properties**, apply named **text styles**, embed **inline images**, track font usage with the Resource Manager, and use proofing options such as **AutoSpell/Spell Checker**, **Proof Reader**, and **Thesaurus**.

- However, tables don't support importing text from a file, editing text with WritePlus or viewing it with the Text Manager, or wrapping text around objects. And table text doesn't flow or link the way frame text does; the Frame context bar's text-fitting functions aren't applicable.

- Tables also have a number of unique features like **AutoFormat, QuickClear and QuickFill** for rapid editing and revision.

- Filter effects can be applied to all of your table text simultaneously—apply **shadows, glow, bevel, emboss,** and **colour fills**. Note that filter effects cannot be applied on a per cell basis.

- Microsoft Excel spreadsheet contents can be pasted directly onto a selected cells within your PagePlus table.

To create a table:

1. Choose the **Table Tool** from the Table flyout on the Tools toolbar and click on the page or pasteboard, or drag to set the table's dimensions. The **Create Table** dialog appears with a selection of preset layouts.

2. Step through the list to preview the layouts and select one.

3. Click **OK** to display the new table on the page.

Manipulating tables

Once you've created a table, you can select, move, resize, delete, and copy an object, just as you can with a text frame. **Cell properties** can also be modified.

To manipulate the table object:

- To select the table object, click its bounding box. Now you can resize it like a text frame by dragging a node, or move it by dragging an edge.

- To delete the table object, select it and press the **Delete** key, or select any part of its text and choose **Delete** from the Table menu (**Table/Delete** from the right-click menu), then **Table** (or **All**) from the submenu. You can also choose **Delete Object** from the Edit menu.

- To duplicate the table object and its text, first make sure no text is selected (an insertion point is OK), then use the **Copy** and **Paste** commands. As a shortcut, select the object and drag with the **Ctrl** key down.

To select and edit text in cells, rows, and columns:

- To select a cell, click for an insertion point or drag to select text. To select more than one cell, click in one cell and drag across the others, one row or column at a time.

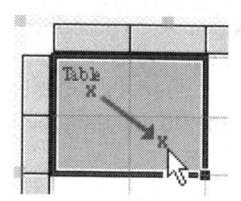

- To move to the next or previous cells, use the keyboard arrow keys, or the **Tab** or **Shift+Tab**) key.

- To enter text, simply type into a cell at the insertion point. Cells expand vertically as you type to accommodate extra lines of text. To enter a Tab character, press **Ctrl+Tab**.

- To select a row or column, click its control button along the left or top of the table. To select more than one row or column, drag across their control buttons.

- To select all text (all rows and columns), choose **Select** from the Table menu, then **All** from the submenu.

- To copy, paste and delete selected table text, use the **Copy**, **Paste** and **Delete** commands as you would for frame text. Alternatively, drag the bottom corner of a selected cell to copy its table text to any of the newly selected cells.

- To format selected text, apply **character and paragraph properties** or **text styles** as with any text.

- To rotate selected text, right-click and choose **Table>Cell Properties**. In the **Orientation** tab, use the rotation dial to set a rotation angle or enter a specific value into the input box.

- Table text shares default properties with frame text. For details, see **Default text properties** on p. 89.

To change the table's structure and appearance:

- To adjust row or column size, drag the line separating control buttons. Note that you can adjust a row's height independent of the amount of text it contains.

- To delete one or more rows or columns, select them (or cell text), then choose **Delete** from the Table menu (**Table>Delete** from the right-click menu), then either **Row(s)** or **Column(s)** from the submenu.

- To insert new rows or columns, select one or more cells as described above, then choose **Insert** from the Table menu (**Table>Insert** from the right-click menu), then either **Rows...** or **Columns...** from the submenu. In the dialog, specify how many to add, and whether to add them before or after the selected cells.

- To merge cells into larger cells that span more than one row or column (for example, a column head), select a range of cells and choose **Merge Cells** from the Table menu (**Table>Merge Cells** from the right-click menu). The merged cell displays only the text originally visible in the top left selected cell. The original cells and their text are preserved, however—to restore them, select the merged cell and choose **Separate Cells** from the Table menu (**Table>Separate Cells** from the right-click menu).

- To copy cell contents (including text, formatting, borders, and colours) to a new location in the same table, select the cell(s), press the Shift key and drag the bottom right-hand corner of the selection to the new location then release. To copy cell contents from one table to another table select the cells, right-click on a cell selection and choose **Copy**—select the area (of the same dimension) in the new table then select **Paste**.

- To move cell contents within the same table, select cells, and when the cursor is displayed, drag the cell(s) to the new location.

Using AutoFormat

To use style presets to customise the table's appearance:

- Choose **AutoFormat...** from the Table menu. The dialog presents a list of sample tables, which differ in their use of **Lines** (inner and outer cell borders), **Fill** (cell fill), **Font** (bold, italic, etc.), and **Alignment** (left, centre, etc.).

- You can pick any sample and use the checkboxes to specify which of the sample's attribute(s) to apply to your actual table. This lets you "mix and match," for example by applying (in two passes) the Colour from one sample and the Font from another.

- To restore plain formatting, choose **Default**.

Setting Cell Properties

To customise the appearance of one or more cells "by hand":

1. Select the cell(s) and choose **Cell Properties...** from the Table menu.
2. Use the dialog's **Border**, **Fill**, **Transparency** and **Margin** tabs to apply cell formatting, then click **OK**.

Using QuickClear and QuickFill

QuickClear and **QuickFill** are handy shortcuts built into tables. Both employ the small "QuickFill handle" which you may have noticed at the lower right of each selected cell (or range of cells).

Jan   ─ QuickFill handle

QuickClear lets you instantly clear a range of cells whereas **QuickFill** lets you quickly enter a standard sequence of numbers or entries, for example the months of the year, the days of the week, or any arithmetic progression (see below). You can also use QuickFill to replicate one cell's contents over a range of cells.

To QuickClear a range of cells:

1. Select the range to be cleared..
2. Drag the QuickFill handle upward until no cells are specified.

To QuickFill a sequence of entries:

1. Type the first entry of the sequence into the starting cell.
2. Drag the selected cell's QuickFill handle out to the range of cells to be quickfilled, as shown below. The function works both backwards and forwards!

If there are not enough items in the QuickFill sequence, the entries wrap back to the beginning value in the sequence.

To replicate a cell's contents over a range of cells:

1. Click to select the cell whose contents you want to replicate.
2. Drag out the cell's QuickFill handle over the range you want to fill.

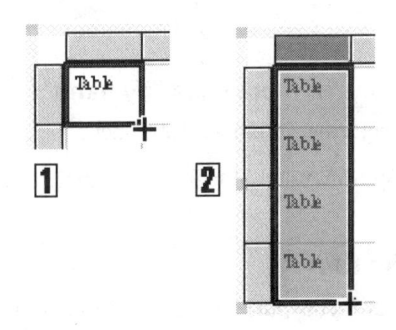

The sequences that QuickFill knows about are:

- January, February, March, ...
- JANUARY, FEBRUARY, MARCH, ...
- january, february, march, ...
- Jan, Feb, Mar, ...
- JAN, FEB, MAR, ...
- jan, feb, mar, ...
- Monday, Tuesday, Wednesday, ...
- MONDAY, TUESDAY, WEDNESDAY, ...
- monday, tuesday, wednesday, ...
- Mon, Tue, Wed, ...
- MON, TUE, WED, ...
- mon, tue, wed, ...
- a, b, c, ...
- A, B, C, ...
- Any arithmetic progression, that is, any series of numbers with a common difference.

For **numerical sequences**, if the starting selection contains two or more cells, QuickFill uses the difference between them as the common difference. For example, if the first two cells contain the numbers 10 and 20, then the 'quickfilled' sequence would be: 10, 20, 30, ... If only a single number is specified, then the common difference between the numbers will be 1.

Similarly, for **non-numerical sequences**, you can specify a step between any entries, for example, enter "January" in the first cell, "March" in the second. QuickFill will place every other month in the sequence: "January, March, May, July, ..."

You can type also phrases including **known sequences**, and QuickFill will fill the sequence, along with the other words. For example, type "Week 1" and QuickFill would give you the sequence "Week 1, Week 2, Week 3, ..." or "Jan Sales" would give: "Jan Sales, Feb Sales, Mar Sales, ..."

Formatting numbers

The Table toolbar includes additional buttons, switched on with the **Spreadsheet functions** button, which let you vary how numbers are displayed. Number formats let you add commas and currency signs to numbers, express numbers as percents, control how many decimal places are displayed, etc. Number formats **do not** alter numbers internally—only the way numbers are displayed.

- Click the **Remove Formatting** button to remove any formatting.

- Click the **Currency** button to apply the currency format and symbol for your locale as suggested by Windows.

- Click the **Percent** button to convert a number to a percentage (multiply by 100 and append a percent sign).

- Click the **Comma** button to separate thousands by a comma and remove decimal places.

- Click the **Increase Decimal** or **Decrease Decimal** button to extend or reduce the number of decimal places shown.

For additional number formatting options:

- Click the **Custom Format** button.

The Custom Formatting dialog appears. Here you can select from any of the listed formats, construct custom formats (with colour for negative values, if you wish), and customise the list. The built-in list includes two currency symbol characters (one positive, one negative) for your locale, as supplied by Windows.

Inserting formulas

A table cell can display the result of a **formula** combining values of other cells with arithmetic operators and functions. Formulas are recalculated whenever values in the table change, so they're always up to date.

Any cell starting with the character "=" is treated as a formula. To enter or edit formulas, use the Table toolbar's edit field. Note that you can only select or edit an entire formula, not just part of it.

To display a cell's formula for editing in the Table toolbar's edit field:

- Click to select the cell containing the formula.

To enter a formula:

- Click the **Function** button on the Table toolbar and choose a specific function from the drop-down menu.

    For example, if you start with a blank cell and choose **SUM()**, PagePlus adds "=SUM()" to the edit field and positions the text cursor between the brackets so that you can type numbers or cell references straight away.

OR

- Click the **Function** button once to seed the edit field with an equal sign (or type "=" yourself), then continue to type the formula.

Click the **Accept** button to update the selected cell.

See the PagePlus Help for a more detailed explanation of formulas.

Inserting a calendar

The **Calendar Wizard** helps you design a month-at-a-glance calendar to use in any publication. You can create a postage-stamp graphic or a full-page "planner." Options include year, month, week and day labelling, room to write, and numerous format options. The calendar is created as a **text-based table** so you can edit it using the standard text tools.

To insert a calendar:

1. Click the **Table** flyout on the Tools toolbar and choose **Insert Calendar** from the submenu.
2. Click again on your page, or drag out to indicate the desired calendar size.

The **Calendar Wizard** then helps you pick a preset and define options for your calendar.

Inserting database tables

As a great way of producing a database report in your publication, it is possible for a database table to be imported and presented as a PagePlus table. The database table could be from one of a comprehensive range of database file formats, as well as from HTML files and various delimited text files.

For a high degree of control, it is also possible to filter and sort your database records prior to import.

To insert a database table:

1. Click the **Table** flyout on the Tools toolbar and choose **Insert Database table** from the submenu.
2. Using the pointer, draw an area on your page that will contain your database information.

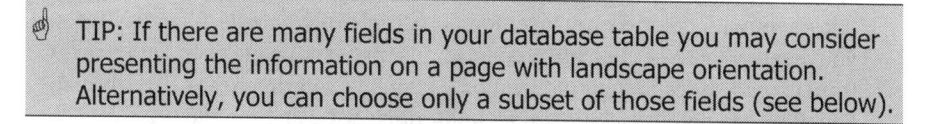

> **TIP:** If there are many fields in your database table you may consider presenting the information on a page with landscape orientation. Alternatively, you can choose only a subset of those fields (see below).

3. In the **Open** dialog, select from the Files of Type drop-down menu the database file that contains the table you require.
4. Navigate to your database file and click **Open**.
5. The **Select Table** dialog displays the tables within your database. Select your table and click OK.
6. The **Merge List** dialog shows all the table rows (records) in the table—choose to **Select All** records, **Toggle Select** (invert all current selections) or use a custom **Filter...**
7. The list of fields available in the table are shown in the **Select Fields** dialog. Uncheck any fields that you don't want to be included in the import process. Again, Select All or Toggle selection options are available.
8. Click the **OK** button.

Filtering your records

Records can be filtered by using the Filter Records tab then subsequently sorted into any combination with the Sort Records tab. The Filter option helps you limit the number of records imported to only those you require.

For example, only records from people living in London with an interest in Ice hockey could be included for import, i.e.

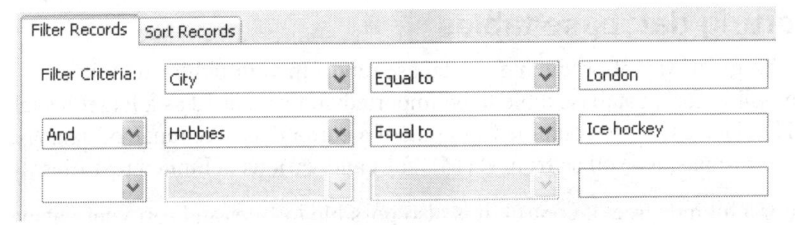

Filter Records	Sort Records		
Filter Criteria:	City	Equal to	London
And	Hobbies	Equal to	Ice hockey

Note that the Boolean operator "And" used to include both terms (as in this example). If the "Or" operator was used records from either London or Ice hockey would be included for import.

The Sort Records tab is used to sort by three prioritised field names, either in ascending or descending order.

Creating a table of contents

A **table of contents** is a useful addition to a **book**, a longer newsletter, or any document with complex organization. The Table of Contents Wizard helps you create a table of contents with headings up to six levels deep, derived from named styles in your publication. If you're exporting to the PDF format, PagePlus can automatically build a **bookmark list** using the same style markings in your text.

To create a table of contents:

1. Decide which named styles you want to designate as headings at each of up to six levels.
2. Check your publication to make sure these styles are used consistently.
3. Review the choices you'll need to make when you run the Table of Contents Wizard.
4. Choose **Table of Contents...** from the Insert menu to run the Wizard.
5. You can easily modify the look of your table of contents, or run the Wizard again to update the information.

Using styles to prepare a table of contents

The Wizard will show you a list of all the style names used in your publication, and you will check boxes to include text of a given style as a heading at a particular level (1 through 6). For example, you could pull out all text using the "Heading" style as your first-level headings.

Entries in the resulting table of contents will appear in the order the text occurs in your publication.

When the table of contents is created, PagePlus formats it using built-in **text styles** intended specifically for table of contents preparation: "Contents-Title" and "Contents-1st" through "Contents-6th". You can easily change the look of your table of contents by changing the style definitions for these built-in "Contents" styles.

Changing the look of your table of contents:

You can update the built-in Contents styles as needed, as explained in **Using text styles** on p. 89.

Creating an index

An **index** is a valuable reader aid in a longer document such as a report or manual. The Index Wizard helps you create an index with **main entries** and **subentries**, based on **index entry marks** you insert.

Marking index entries

1. Choose **Edit Story** from the File menu.
2. Select the term to be included in the index, or click for an insertion point just before the word where the index mark should go.
3. Click the **Mark Index** button from the Story Toolbar.
4. Use the **Mark Index Entry** dialog to insert or edit index entry marks.

> NOTE: Index entry marks are invisible on the PagePlus screen and can only be added or edited in WritePlus.

If you selected a word or phrase in the story, it appears as the main entry in the dialog. You can use the entry as it is, or type new text for the main entry and sub-entry (if any). You must include a main entry for each sub-entry. The dialog's scrolling list records entries and sub-entries alphabetically.

- To reuse an entry, click it in the list.
- For a standard index entry, leave the **Current page** box checked.
- To insert a cross-reference with the term(s) preceded by "See:", select **Cross-reference** (to include a word other than "See," simply replace it in the box).

- You can also specify a bold and/or italic page number format.
- Click **Mark** to insert the new entry mark or update a selected mark.
- To undo a mark entry, click the **Undo** button or press **Ctrl+Z**.

To build an index:

First mark the entries as described above. Then in PagePlus...

1. Review the choices you'll need to make before running the Index Wizard (see below).
2. Choose **Index...** from the Insert menu.

You can easily modify the look of your index, or run the Wizard again to update the information.

Changing the look of your index:

You can update the built-in Index styles (Index-Title, -Separator, -Main, and -Sub) as needed, as explained in the **Using text styles** on p. 89. For example, indent the "Index-Sub" text slightly, and introduce some space above the "Index-Separator" text.

Producing a book with BookPlus

BookPlus is a management utility built into PagePlus that lets you produce a whole book—a collection of chapters—from a set of separate PagePlus (*.PPP) publication files. Using BookPlus, you can arrange the chapter files in a specific order, systematically **renumber** pages, **synchronise** styles and other elements between all chapters, create a **Table of Contents and/or Index** for the whole book, and **output** the book via printing, PostScript®, or PDF. BookPlus can perform all these managerial tasks whether or not the original files are open! Your settings are saved as a compact BookPlus (*.PPB) book file, separate from the source publication files.

Working with books and chapters

A book consists of a set of PagePlus (*.PPP) publication files. Each publication file is considered a chapter in the book. In order to create a new book, you'll first need at least one constituent chapter file.

> NOTE: Be sure to define similar page setup options (such as dimensions and facing page structure) for each chapter, as BookPlus will not override these publication-level settings.

To create a new book:

- In PagePlus, choose **New** from the File menu and select **New Book...** from the submenu.

BookPlus opens with an empty central region reserved for the **chapter list**.

To add a chapter to the chapter list:

1. In BookPlus, choose **Add...** from the Chapter menu.
2. In the dialog, select one or more PagePlus files to be added as chapters. (Use the **Ctrl** or **Shift** keys to select multiple files or a range of files.) Click **Open**.

The selected files appear in the chapter list.

> NOTE: Once you've created a chapter list, you can add new chapters at any time, or replace/remove chapters in the current list (see below).

To reorder chapters in the list:

- Drag a chapter file's name (in the Chapter column) to the desired position.

To open one or more chapter files for editing:

- Double-click a specific chapter name in the Chapter column.
  OR

- Select one or more chapter names and choose **Open** from the Chapter menu.

The selected file(s) open in PagePlus. In BookPlus, any open chapters are listed as "Open" in the Status column.

To replace or remove a chapter file:

- Select its name in the list and choose **Replace...** or **Remove** from the Chapter menu.

The Remove command deletes the chapter from the list. The Replace command displays a dialog that lets you select another file to be substituted into the same position in the list.

> NOTE: Replace is useful if a file has been moved or externally modified and you need to update the BookPlus listing. Neither command affects the original file. Only the chapter list is updated.

To save the current chapter list as a book file:

- Choose **Save** (or **Save As...**) from the BookPlus File menu.

> NOTE: You can open saved book files from PagePlus using **File/Open...**. You can have more than one book file open at a time.

Numbering pages in BookPlus

BookPlus provides a variety of options for incrementing page numbers continuously from one chapter to another, through the whole book. Of course, page numbers will only appear on pages or (more commonly) master pages where you've inserted page number fields. To "suppress" page numbers—for example, on a title page—simply don't include a page number field there.

BookPlus lets you change page number style choices you've made in the original file (using **Format/Page Number Format...** in PagePlus), and provides other options such as inserting a blank page when necessary to force new chapters to start on a right-hand page. You don't need to have the original files open to update page numbering.

To set page numbering options for the book:

1. Choose **Book Page Number Options...** from the BookPlus File menu.
2. In the dialog, select whether you want page numbers to **Continue from previous chapter**, **Continue on next odd page**, or **Continue on next even page**. Typically you'll want new chapters to start on odd (right-hand or "recto") pages.
3. Leave **Insert blank page when necessary** checked if you want to output an extra page at the end of a chapter where the next page number (if you've selected odd- or even-page continuation) would otherwise skip a page. Either way, BookPlus will number your pages correctly—but for correct imposition in professional printing it's usually best to insert the blank page. You won't see any blank page inserted in your original file, only in the generated output.
4. Click **OK**, and BookPlus immediately applies your settings to all chapters.

To set page numbering options for a chapter:

1. Select its name in the list and choose **Chapter Page Number Options...** from the Chapter menu. The dialog displays current settings for numbering scheme and initial numbering.
2. To change the numbering scheme, make a selection in the Style section. For example, you might use lowercase Roman numerals for a preface.

3. To force page numbering to start at a certain value, uncheck **Continue from previous chapter** and type the starting value. For example, you might want to skip page numbering for introductory ("front") matter and begin numbering from "1" on the first page of main body text.

4. Click **OK**, and BookPlus immediately applies your settings to the selected chapter. These settings only apply to the selected chapter.

If you've reordered chapters or changed the chapter list in any way, you can quickly reimpose correct numbering on the current list.

To update page numbering:

- Choose **Renumber Pages** from the BookPlus File menu.

Synchronising chapters

Synchronising means imposing consistent styles, palettes, and/or colour schemes throughout the book. This is easily accomplished by using one chapter (called the **style source**) as a model for the rest of the book. You define attributes in the style source chapter, and then select which attributes should be adjusted in other chapters to conform to the style source. For example, you could redefine the "Normal" text style in your style source chapter, then quickly propagate that change through the rest of the book. The Modified and Synchronised columns of the BookPlus chapter list let you keep track of recent file changes.

To set one chapter as the style source:

- Select its name in the chapter list and choose **Set Style Source** from the Chapter menu.

The current style source is identified in the Synchronized column of the chapter list.

To synchronise one or more chapters with the style source:

1. To update just certain chapters, make sure their names are selected in the chapter list.

2. Choose **Synchronise...** from the File menu.

3. In the dialog, select whether you want to update **All** or just **Selected** chapters. Check which attributes should be updated to conform to those defined in the style source file: **Text styles**, **Object styles**, **Colour scheme**, and/or **Colour palette**.

4. Click **OK**.

BookPlus imposes the specified changes and updates the Synchronised time in the chapter list for each selected file. If the file was altered in any way, the Modified time updates as well.

> NOTE: Synchronising does not alter footnote or endnote numbering.

Building a Table of Contents or Index

From BookPlus, you can build a **Table of Contents** and/or **Index** that includes entries for the entire set of chapters. In each case, you'll need to begin by designating a specific chapter where the resulting pages should be added. Otherwise the steps are identical to those detailed in the main topics, as noted below.

To create a table of contents or index for the book:

1. Complete basic preparatory steps as described in **Creating a table of contents** or **Creating an index** on p. 116 or 117, respectively.
2. In the chapter list, select the name of the chapter file where you want to add the table of contents or index.
3. Choose **Insert** from the Chapter menu and select **Table of Contents...** or **Index...** from the submenu.

BookPlus opens the chapter file if it's not already open, and the Wizard for the procedure you've selected appears.

4. Select **Yes** when the Wizard asks if you want to build a table of contents or index for the entire book. Continue clicking **Next>** and selecting choices in the Wizard.

Printing and PDF output

When you **print** or generate **PDF output** from BookPlus, you'll have the choice of printing the entire book or selected chapters. Otherwise the steps are identical to those detailed in the main topics, as noted below.

To print the book or selected chapters:

1. To print just certain chapters, make sure their names are selected in the chapter list.
2. Choose **Print...** from the BookPlus File menu.

3. Under "Print Range" on the General tab, select **Entire book** to output all chapters, or **Selected chapters** to output just those you selected. You can also select the **Pages** option to output one or more specific page(s). Whichever option you've chosen, a drop-down list lets you export all sheets in the range, or just odd or even sheets.
   Note: If you select **Print to file** to output PostScript, BookPlus will generate a separate file for each chapter.

4. Set other options as detailed in Printing basics on p. 185, then click **Print**.

To export the book or selected chapters as PDF:

1. To export just certain chapters, make sure their names are selected in the chapter list.

2. Choose **Publish as PDF...** from the BookPlus File menu.

3. Under "Print Range" on the General tab, select **Entire book** to output all chapters, or **Selected chapters** to output just those you selected. You can also select the **Pages** option to output one or more specific page(s). Whichever option you've chosen, a drop-down list lets you export all pages in the range, or just odd or even pages.

4. Set other options as detailed in Exporting PDF files on p. 193, then click **OK**.

Using mail merge

Mail merge means printing your publication a number of times, inserting different information each time from a **data source** such as an address list file—for example into a series of letters or mailing labels. It is even possible to merge picture data (for example, digital photos) into single fields or even auto-create a grid layout of pictures and text suitable for catalogs or photo albums.

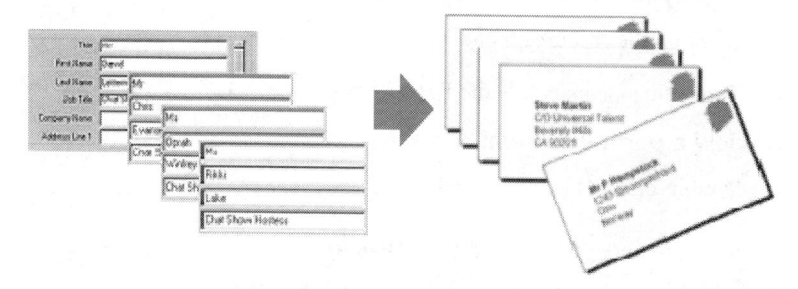

As mail merge is an advanced feature of PagePlus, see the PagePlus Help which covers mail merge in more detail. Subjects covered include:

- Opening a data source
- Editing Serif Database files
- Selecting, filtering, and sorting the merge list
- Inserting placeholders for your data
- Previewing data in the publication
- Merging and printing

Checking fonts and resources used

The **Resource Manager** lists the fonts and resources used in your publication, and shows if the pictures are linked to external picture files or embedded within the document. In addition, it will allow font substitution after import of PDF or opening of PagePlus files; this is necessary when fonts used in the publications are not available on your PC.

To display the Resource Manager:

- Choose **Resource Manager...** from the Tools menu.

Checking resources

The Resources tab lists imported pictures, media, Java applets, etc and their current status. It shows whether each is linked or embedded and lets you switch a resource from one mode to the other. "Linked" data consists of a reference to the original file. If you copy or move a publication with linked resources, for example from one computer to another, you should also copy any resource files linked to the publication.

To display the path name for a resource:

- Click on the resource name.
- The path appears below the Resources section.

To view a particular item:

- Double-click its name in the list.
  OR
  Select the item's name and click **Display**.

To switch an item from linked to embedded:

1. Select the item's name.
2. Click **Embed** to embed a linked item.

Conversely, click **Make Linked** to link an embedded item.

To check whether pictures you import are to be linked or embedded:

- Choose **Options...** from the Tools menu and click the **General** tab.

- Check **Suggest embed/link picture** for embedding or linking. Set a file size below which files are embedded automatically.

Checking fonts

The Fonts tab lists fonts used in text objects on individual pages or throughout the whole publication, along with their current status. The status column can display "OK" or "Missing". If "Missing" is shown then the font is not available on your PC. For this reason, if you are copying a publication to take to a different computer, you should check that the fonts used are available on the new computer.

A third column called Substitutions shows which local fonts are being used as substitutes for missing fonts.

To display the font category:

- Click on the font name.

The font category (TrueType, Printer, or System) appears below the Fonts section.

To view a particular item:

- Double-click its name in the list.
  OR
  Select the item's name and click **Display**.

Substituting fonts

Font substitution issues may arise when opening PagePlus Publications (*.PPP) and importing PDF files. This is because the original fonts used within the publication may not be present on the target PC. If this occurs, font substitution will take place automatically when the .PPP or .PDF file is opened. This is indicated by the message "*Publication uses fonts which are no longer available. Substitute fonts will be used*".

PagePlus's font substitution mechanism makes use of the PANOSE Font Matching System which intelligently (and automatically) finds the best font substitution match between a missing and a locally available font.

> NOTE: Serif PagePlus does not make use of embedded fonts present in imported PDFs.

> NOTE: If a font is unavailable and has been substituted, its font name on the Context Bar is prefixed by the "?" character.

From this point, three options are open to you:

- continue with the fonts substituted on import.
- install the original fonts.
- swap the fonts substituted on import with fonts of your choosing.

The last option is carried out via PagePlus's **Resource Manager**, designed for font management. The Fonts tab is used for font substitution via a **Substitute Missing Fonts** dialog.

The dialog allows missing fonts to be replaced by available fonts selected from a font list. The available fonts are those currently installed on your PC. It's also possible to add more than one font to act as a replacement, which is particularly useful if you want to provide an alternative to your first choice substituted font, e.g. a more widely available font such as Verdana, Arial or Times New Roman could act as a secondary font.

Clearly, the process of substituting large numbers of fonts is time-consuming, a challenge to the memory and most importantly document specific only. As a solution, especially if the same substitutions need to be applied between different publications in the future, you can export all your font mappings to a single Serif Font Map (*.SFM) file which can subsequently be imported into other publications—saving you the effort of recreating the mappings again. The SFM file replaces the font mapping information stored within the publication.

> NOTE: The font map file is binary so cannot be edited.

For each font substitution in the **Substitute Missing Fonts** dialog, the mappings shown in the Substitute with box can be reset to default by clicking the **Default** button. This will replace the fonts listed with a single font, e.g. Arial or Times New Roman, as governed by Windows (this is not configurable).

To substitute a font:

1. Select **Resource Manager** from the Tools menu.
2. Choose the **Fonts** tab, and select the **Substitutions** button.
3. In the dialog, select a missing font from the **Font to substitute** drop-down menu.
4. Choose a replacement font from the Available fonts list box ensuring that the **Bold** and/or **Italic** options are checked if necessary. Some fonts may be a more acceptable substitute with the bold or italic style set.
5. Click **Add<<** to place the font in the **Substitute with** box. This box can contain more than one font—your first choice and a secondary font (e.g. Arial or Times New Roman). You should always place your first choice at the top of the list with the **Move up** or **Move down** buttons.
6. Go back to Step 3 and substitute each missing font in the **Font to substitute** drop-down menu in turn.

To export Serif Font Map files:

1. Perform font mappings for all missing fonts as described above.
2. Select the **Export** button.
3. Save your font substitutions to a Serif Font Map (SFM) file in a chosen location.

To import Serif Font Map files:

1. Open a publication to which you want to apply saved font substitutions.
2. Select **Resource Manager** from the Tools menu.
3. Choose the **Fonts** tab, and select the **Substitutions** button.
4. Select the **Import** button.
5. Locate the Serif Font Map (SFM) file, select it and click **Open**.

Saved substitutions in the Font Map file are applied to the current publication.

For PDF imports especially, if you want all new publications to utilise the font substitutions used in your current publication, use the **Tools>Save Defaults** option to make the current font substitutions your default.

Working with Images, Lines and Shapes

6

Importing images

PagePlus lets you insert images from a wide variety of file formats. Here's a quick overview:

- **Bitmapped** images, also known as **bitmaps** or **raster** images, are built from a matrix of dots ("pixels"), rather like the squares on a sheet of graph paper. They may originate as digital camera photos or scanned images, or be created (or enhanced) with a "paint" program or photo editor.

- **Draw** graphics, also known as **vector** images, are resolution-independent and contain drawing commands such as "draw a line from A to B.".

- **Metafiles** are the native graphics format for Windows and combine raster and vector information.

You can also acquire images directly from PhotoCDs or via TWAIN devices (scanners or digital cameras).

Inserting images

There are several ways to bring an image into PagePlus. Decide in advance where you want to place the picture, and whether to insert it by embedding or by linking.

- **Detached** images float freely on a page, while **inline** images are incorporated with the text flow in a text object.

- **Embedded** images become part of the publication file, while **linking** places a reference copy of the image on the page and preserves a connection to the original file. Each approach has its pros and cons (see **Embedding vs. Linking** on p. 133).

- **Picture frames:** You also have the option of creating an empty **picture frame** as a placeholder and then later on importing an image into it. Not to be confused with a decorative **border**, a picture frame is a container akin to a text frame. The frame itself can be either detached or inline, and at any time you can swap a different image into the same frame. This gives you the flexibility of separating the container from its content—you can incorporate the picture frame into your layout irrespective of the actual picture that will go inside it.

To import an image from a file:

1. If you want to place the image inline, click for an insertion point in a text object. For a detached image, make sure text objects are deselected. To put the image in a frame, create the frame (see above) and select it.

2. **In the main window:**

   1. Click the **Import Picture** button on the Tools toolbar's Picture flyout.

   2. To replace an existing picture, select it and click the **Replace Picture** button on the Picture context bar.

   In WritePlus:

   - Choose **Picture File...** from the Insert menu.

3. Use the dialog to select the image file to open. Check **Preview** to examine images in the window at right.

4. If you check the **Place at native dpi** option and the image has a different internal setting, PagePlus will scale the image accordingly; otherwise it applies a screen resolution setting of **96 dpi**. Either way—or if you resize it downwards later on—the image retains all its original picture data until it's published.

5. Select either **Embed Picture** or **Link Picture**.

6. Click **Open**.

7. If there's a text insertion point in the main window, you'll be prompted whether to insert the image at the current cursor position. Click **Yes** if that's what you want.

8. If there was no insertion point (or you answer "No" to the insertion prompt), you'll see the mouse pointer change to the Picture Paste cursor. What you do next determines the initial size and placement of the detached image.

9. To insert the picture at a default size, simply click the mouse.
   OR
   To set the size of the inserted picture, drag out a region and release the mouse button.

Embedding vs. linking

Embedding means the image in PagePlus is now distinct from the original file. Embedding results in a larger PagePlus file, and if you need to alter an embedded image you'll need to re-import it after editing. Still, it's the best choice if file size isn't an issue and graphics are final.

Linking inserts a copy of the image file into the PagePlus publication, linked to the actual file so that any changes you later make to it in the native application will be automatically reflected in PagePlus. Linking is one way of avoiding "bloat" by limiting the size of the publication file. On the other hand, you'll need to manage the externally linked files carefully, for example making sure to include them all if you move the PagePlus file to a different drive.

By default, PagePlus prompts you to embed pictures that are smaller than 256K, by preselecting the "Embed Picture" option in the Insert Picture dialog (but you can always select "Link Picture" instead). If you like, you can change the threshold file size or even switch off the automatic selection.

You can use the Resource Manager later on, to change an item's status from linked to embedded, or vice versa.

To preselect embedding or linking based on file size:

1. Choose **Options...** from the Tools menu. You'll see the **General** tab.
2. To preselect the "Embed Picture" option for images under a certain size, select the threshold size in the "Embed if smaller than" list. ("Link Picture" will be preselected for images larger than the threshold.)
3. To choose whether to embed or link each image, uncheck **Suggest embed/link picture**. You can still select either option in the import dialog; it will now remember and preselect the last setting you used.

Applying adjustments

The **Picture context bar** appears automatically when you select an image on the page. You can use it to improve the appearance of any image appearing in your publication by adjusting contrast, brightness, colour, and size directly, or by applying **Image adjustments**.

PagePlus comes equipped with a powerful mix of colour correction/ adjustment tools for use on your newly imported images. Levels, colour balance, channel mixer, red eye and HSL corrective adjustments, amongst others, are available.

Effect-inducing adjustments also range from the artistic Diffuse Glow to the more practical correction methods such as Dust and Scratch Remover. In fact over 20 adjustments can be directly applied to your image not only individually but cumulatively.

Adjustments are managed by using the **Image Adjustments** dialog. The gallery offers a one-stop shop for applying your adjustments all supported by a dynamic preview window!

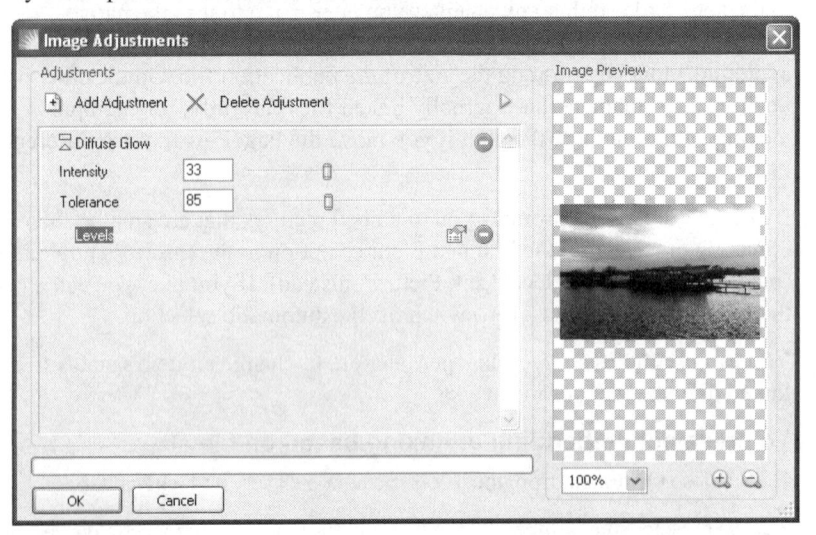

> NOTE: Adjustments and effects can be applied to imported pictures as well as objects converted to pictures within PagePlus.

If you're looking to carry our some more advanced photo editing and have Serif's PhotoPlus software (10 or above) installed, you can use the **Edit in PhotoPlus** button on the Picture context bar. You can carry out your edit and save the file in PhotoPlus if embedded or linked, such that the newly altered image is refreshed and updated in PagePlus automatically.

> TIP: You can also embed a **Serif PhotoPlus Picture** (*.SPP) file directly into PagePlus, and make edits to it in PhotoPlus as above.

Adding an adjustment or effect

Adding an adjustment is as easy as choosing an option from a drop-down menu in the Image Adjustments dialog. To assist in the selection of an appropriate adjustment the list is separated into corrective adjustments (in the first half of the list), and effect-inducing adjustments (in the second half). As soon as an adjustment is selected it is added to a stack where additional adjustments can be added and built up by using the same method. Any adjustment can be switched on/off, deleted or reordered in this list. The order in which they appear in the stack may produce very different results—if you're not happy with your current order—PagePlus lets you drag and drop your adjustment into any position in the stack.

Adjustments are applied in the same way that PagePlus layers are applied, i.e. the first applied always appears at the bottom of the list and is applied to the picture first. In the above example, the Diffuse Glow effect is applied first, then Levels next.

To add an image adjustment:

1. Select the picture that you want to apply an adjustment to.
2. Click the **Image Adjustments** button on the Picture context bar.
3. In the Image Adjustments dialog, click the **Add Adjustment** button.
4. From the drop-down menu select an adjustment.
5. There are three methods to configure properties depending on the adjustment selected: Adjust the properties of the adjustment by moving the sliders or entering different values into the input boxes.
   OR
   For more complex adjustments, make changes in a pop-up dialog.

> NOTE: Some adjustments have no properties and are applied directly as they are selected.

6. Click the **OK** button.

Add more than one adjustment to the picture by repeating the above procedure.

Switching on/off adjustments and effects

In the same way in which a layer's contents can be made visible/invisible, the **Disable** button can be used to temporarily make an adjustment invisible or visible.

Modifying adjustments and effects

The properties of any selected adjustment can be changed in one of two ways:

- Properties will be displayed alongside the adjustment in the stack (in Image Adjustments dialog)—you can alter and experiment with these.

- The properties of an applied effect or adjustment can be changed by clicking the **Properties** button alongside the effect (in the Image Adjustments dialog) this is because some effects are more complex to modify by their nature and require to be presented in a separate dialog.

Reordering adjustments and effects

Adjustments can be moved around the stack to change the order in which they are applied to the picture. Drag a name to another position in the list while holding down the mouse button. A dark line indicates the new position in which the entry will be place if the mouse button is released.

Multiple adjustments and effects

It's quite possible to apply several adjustments to the same image, and, depending on the order in which they are applied, to end up with a different final result.

Using the Gallery

The **Gallery** tab serves as a container for storing your own design objects (such as pictures, text blocks, even unlinked text frames or HTML fragments) you'd like to reuse in different publications. It also includes sample designs and (when you install the *PagePlus 11 Resource CD*) is stocked with a wide variety of predesigned elements that you can customise and use as a starting point for your own designs. Once you've copied a design to the Gallery, it becomes available in any publication—simply open the Gallery!

To view the Gallery tab:

- The **Gallery** tab is by default docked with other tabs. If not displayed, go to **View>Studio Tabs** and select the **Gallery** tab.

The Gallery has two parts: (1) an upper **Categories** group and (2) a lower **Designs** group where you drag designs for storage. The Designs group shows a list of thumbnails representing the designs in the selected category.

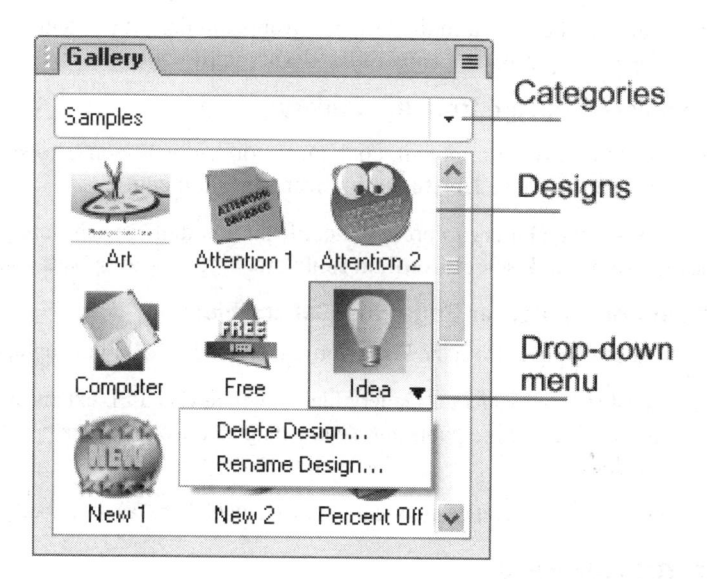

You can maintain your own collection of Gallery designs by adding and deleting items, with the option of naming individual elements to facilitate rapid access.

Each design in the design group can be deleted or renamed from a drop-down menu, available by clicking in the bottom right-hand corner of any design.

To add, delete, or rename Gallery categories:

1. With the Gallery tab selected, click the ▷ **Options** button and choose **Add category**, **Remove category**, or **Rename category** from the drop-down list.
2. Use the dialog to enter and/or confirm your change.

To move or copy an object into the Gallery:

1. To move, drag the object from the page and drop it onto the Designs group in the right category. To copy, press the **Ctrl** key before starting to drag.
2. If the **Prompt to Rename** option is turned on, you'll be prompted to type a name for the design. (You can name or rename the design later, if you wish.) By default, unnamed designs are labelled as "Unnamed."

138 | Working with Images, Lines and Shapes

3. A thumbnail of the design appears in the Designs group, and its name or label appears below the design.

To use a design from the Gallery:

- Click its thumbnail in the Designs group and drag it out onto the page. The Gallery retains a copy of the design until you expressly delete it.

To delete a design from the Gallery:

- Select a design thumbnail, click on the drop-down icon (shown by hover over) and choose **Delete Design** from the submenu.

If you want the Gallery to present a confirmation dialog each time you delete a design, right-click select **Confirm to delete**. Uncheck to bypass confirmation.

To import an earlier PagePlus Gallery file:

1. Choose **Open...** from the File menu and select the "All Files" option.
2. Locate the old PagePlus Gallery file—it will have a .PPL extension—and open it. The .PPL file is a publication containing all the objects in a particular gallery category.
3. Drag the items you wish to retain into a new Gallery, as described above.

Naming designs

To rename a design:

- Select a design thumbnail, click on the drop-down icon (shown by hover over) and choose **Rename Design** from the submenu. Type the new name and click **OK**. The new name appears immediately underneath the design.

If you want the Gallery to prompt you for a name each time you drag in a new design, check **Prompt to Rename** from the above submenu. Uncheck to bypass the prompt.

Finding designs

To locate a design:

1. Click on ▷ **Options** button for the Gallery tab and choose **Find Design....** from the drop-down menu.
2. Type the text to find and click **Find Next**. Starting from the first item displayed, PagePlus searches for the next design (if any) whose name or text includes the search text. The search spans all your Gallery categories.
3. Click **Find Next** to continue the search, or **Close** to exit.

Drawing and editing lines

PagePlus provides Freehand Line, Straight Line, Curved Line, and QuickShape tools for creating simple graphics. Using the **line tools** (found on a Tools toolbar flyout), you can draw single lines, connect line segments together, or join line ends to **close** the line, creating a **shape** (see **Drawing and editing shapes** on p. 145 for details). Use the Pointer tool and the **Curve context bar** to resize or reshape lines once you've drawn them.

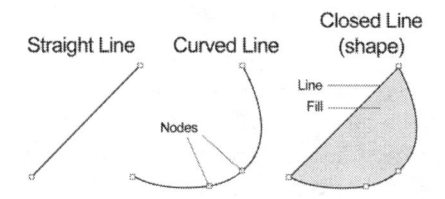

Straight Line   Curved Line   Closed Line (shape)
Nodes   Line   Fill

The **Freehand Line** tool lets you sketch curved lines and shapes in a freeform way.

The **Straight Line** tool is for drawing straight lines (for example, drawn in the column gutter to separate columns); rules at the top and/or bottom of the page; or horizontal lines to separate sections or highlight headlines.

The **Curved Line** tool lets you join a series of line segments (which may be curved or straight) using "connect the dots" mouse clicks.

Drawing lines

To draw a freeform line (with the Freehand Line tool):

1. Click the Line Tools flyout on the Tools toolbar and choose the **Freehand Line tool**.
2. Click where you want the line to start, and hold the mouse button down as you draw. The line appears immediately and follows your mouse movements.
3. To end the line, release the mouse button. The line will automatically smooth out using a minimal number of nodes.

140 | Working with Images, Lines and Shapes   PagePlus 11 User Guide

4. To extend the line, position the cursor over one of its red end nodes. The cursor changes to include a plus symbol. Click on the node and drag to add a new line segment.

To draw a straight line (with the Straight Line tool):

1. Click the Line Tools flyout on the Tools toolbar and choose the **Straight Line tool** from the flyout.

2. Click where you want the line to start, and drag to the end point. The line appears immediately.

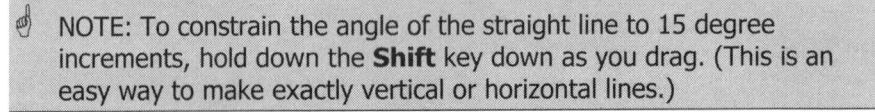

> NOTE: To constrain the angle of the straight line to 15 degree increments, hold down the **Shift** key down as you drag. (This is an easy way to make exactly vertical or horizontal lines.)

3. To extend the line, position the cursor over one of its red end nodes. The cursor changes to include a plus symbol. Click on the node and drag to add a new line segment.

To draw one or more line segments (with the Curved Line tool):

1. Click the Line Tools flyout on the Tools toolbar and choose the **Curved Line tool** from the flyout. The Curve Creation context bar appears, with three buttons that let you select which kind of segment you'll draw next.

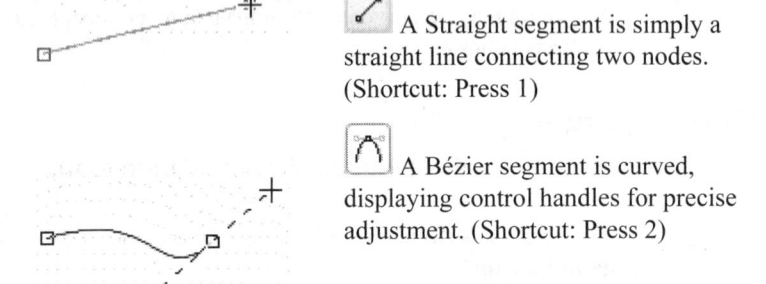

   A Straight segment is simply a straight line connecting two nodes. (Shortcut: Press 1)

   A Bézier segment is curved, displaying control handles for precise adjustment. (Shortcut: Press 2)

Smart segments appear without visible control handles, using automatic curve-fitting to connect each node. They are especially useful when tracing around curved objects and pictures. (Shortcut: Press 3)

2. Select a segment type, then click where you want the line to start.

- For a **Straight** segment, just click again (or drag) for a new node where you want the segment to end. **Shift**-click to align the segment at 15-degree intervals (useful for quick right-angle junctions).

- For a **Bézier** segment, click again for a new node and drag out a **control handle** from it. (Control handles act like "magnets," pulling the curve into shape. The distance between handles determines the depth of the resulting curved line.) Click again where you want the segment to end, and a curved segment appears. Pressing the **Shift** key while you're drawing causes the new node's control handles to "snap" into orientation at 15-degree intervals with respect to the node.

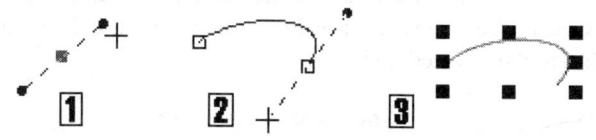

- For a **Smart** segment, click again for a new node. The segment appears as a smooth, best-fitting curve (without visible control handles) between the new node and the preceding node. Before releasing the mouse button, you can drag to "flex" the line as if bending a piece of wire. If the preceding corner node on the line is also smart, flexibility extends back to the preceding segment. You can **Shift**-click to create a new node that lines up at 15-degree intervals with the previous node.

3. To extend an existing line, repeat Step 2 for each new segment. Each segment can be of a different type.

> NOTE: To select the opposite end node of the curve (i.e., to extend the curve from the other end), press **Tab** before drawing the next segment.

4. To end the line, press **Esc**, double-click, or choose a different tool.

You can reshape the line after it's drawn (see below) or apply different weight, colour, or other attributes (see **Setting line properties** on p. 143).

Editing lines

Use the Pointer tool in conjunction with the Curve context bar (see below) to adjust lines once you've drawn them. The techniques are the same whether you're editing a separate line object or the outline of a closed shape.

To move or resize a line:

- Select the line with the Pointer tool and drag its bounding box to move or resize. When resizing, use the **Shift** key if you wish to keep the line constrained.

To reshape a line:

1. Select a line segment with the Pointer tool. You'll see the cursor.
2. Drag the line to reshape it. PagePlus automatically applies curve-smoothing to help you achieve a pleasing result.

Selected node(s) will turn orange, and **control handles** for the adjacent line segment(s) will appear. Note that each segment in the line has a control handle at either end, so when you select an **interior node**, as at left below, you'll see a pair of handles at the selected node.

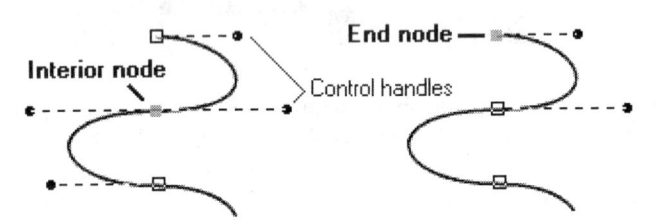

3. Drag the node(s). (**Shift**-drag to constrain the movement to 15-degree intervals.)
   OR
   Adjust one or both of a node's control handles to change the profile of the adjacent segment(s).

Curve context bar

The **Curve context bar** appears when you select a line or closed shape, and provides a variety of adjustment controls—including adding/deleting nodes and manipulation of curves. These are described in the PagePlus Help.

Setting line properties

All lines, including those that enclose shapes, have numerous properties, including colour, weight (width or thickness), scaling, cap (end) and join (corner). You can vary these properties for any freehand, straight, or curved line, as well as for the outline of a shape (see the **Drawing and Editing Shapes** on p. 145). Text frames, tables, and artistic text objects have line properties, too.

To change line properties of a selected object:

- ▣ Use the Swatches tab to change the line's colour and/or shade. (If changing the outline colour of a shape or other object, click the **Line** button so that the line, not the fill, will change.) Click a gallery sample in the tab's Document or standard palettes to apply that colour to the selected object. Alternatively, use the Colour tab to apply a colour to the selected object from a colour mixer.

- Use the Line tab to change the line's weight (thickness), type, or other properties. Select a line width with the slider, and use the drop-down boxes to pick the type of line.

In the Line tab, the middle **Line Styles** drop-down menu provides the following: **None**, **Single**, **Calligraphic**, **Dashed**, and several **Double** line styles.

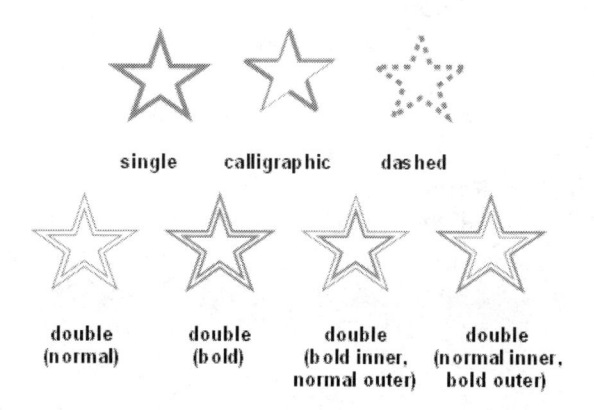

single   calligraphic   dashed

double   double   double   double
(normal)   (bold)   (bold inner,   (normal inner,
                            normal outer)   bold outer)

Several styles provide additional ways to customise the line:

For Dashed lines, drag the Dash Pattern slider to set the overall pattern length (the number of boxes to the left of the slider) and the dash length (the number of those boxes that are black). The illustrations below show lines with pattern and dash lengths of (**1**) 4 and 2, and (**2**) 5 and 4:

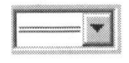

For Double lines, select from one of four **Double** line styles above. Double (normal) is shown in the drop-down menu opposite.

For Calligraphic lines of variable width (drawn as if with a square-tipped pen held at a certain angle), use the **Calligraphic Angle** box to set the angle of the pen tip.

The Line panel also lets you vary a line's **Cap** (end) and the **Join** (corner) where two lines intersect. Both properties tend to be more conspicuous on thicker lines; joins are more apparent with more acute angles. The respective button icons clearly communicate each setting:

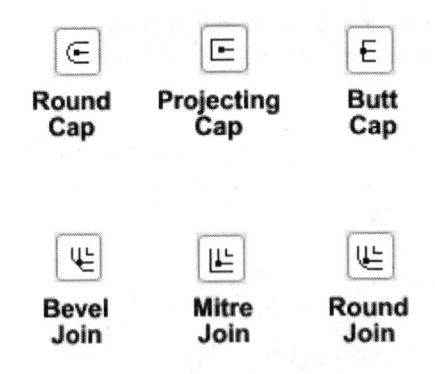

Round Cap   **Projecting Cap**   **Butt Cap**

Bevel Join   **Mitre Join**   **Round Join**

To access all Line properties:

- Click the ![icon] **Line/Border** button on the Tools toolbar's Fill flyout. The Line tab of the Line and Border dialog lets you adjust all line properties.

> NOTE: The Border tab (see **Adding borders** on p. 157) provides a variety of other options for decorative outlines.

- If you want to apply the line to specific edges of the object, use the dialog's Line Edges tab.

Drawing and editing shapes

PagePlus provides Freehand Line, Straight Line, Curved Line, and QuickShape tools for creating simple graphics. **QuickShapes** are pre-designed objects that you can instantly add to your page, then adjust and vary using control handles. Another way of creating shapes is to **draw a line** (or series of line segments) and then connect its start and end nodes, creating a **closed shape**. Once you've drawn a shape, you can adjust its properties—for example, apply **gradient or Bitmap fills** (including your own bitmap pictures!) or apply **transparency effects**.

New shapes take the default line and fill (initially a black line with no fill).

QuickShapes

The QuickShape flyout contains a wide variety of commonly used shapes, including boxes, ovals, arrows, polygons and stars.

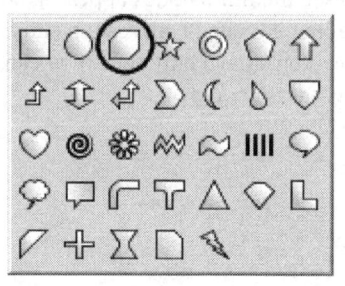

To create a QuickShape:

1. Click the **QuickShape** button on the Tools toolbar and select a shape from the flyout. The button takes on the icon of the shape you selected.
2. Click on the page to create a new shape at a default size. Drag to adjust its dimensions.
3. When the shape is the right size, release the mouse button. Now you can alter the shape by dragging on its handles.

To draw a constrained shape (such as a circle):

- Hold down the **Shift** key as you drag.

All QuickShapes can be **positioned**, **resized**, **rotated**, and **filled**. What's more, you can adjust their designs using the Pointer tool. Each shape changes in a logical way to allow its exact appearance to be altered. The ability to alter the appearance of QuickShape objects makes them more flexible and convenient than clipart pictures with similar designs.

To adjust the appearance of a QuickShape:

1. Select it with the Pointer tool. One or more sliding handles appear next to the shape. Different QuickShapes have different handles.
2. To find out what each handle does for a particular shape, move the Node tool over the handle and read the HintLine.
3. To change the appearance of a QuickShape, drag its handles.

Closed shapes

As soon as you draw or select a line, you'll see the line's nodes appear. Nodes show the end points of each segment in the line. Freehand curves typically have many nodes; straight or curved line segments have only two. You can make a shape by extending a line back to its starting point.

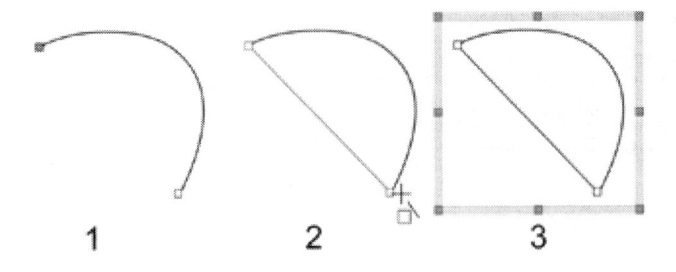

1   2   3

To turn a selected line into a shape:

- Select the line with the Pointer tool and click the ![icon] **Close Curve** button on the Curve context bar.

You can go the other way, too—break open a shape in order to add one or more line segments.

To break open a line or shape:

1. With the Pointer tool, select the node where you want to break the shape.

2. Click the ![icon] **Break Curve** button on the Curve context bar. A line will separate into two lines. A shape will become a line, with the selected node split into two nodes, one at each end of the new line.

3. You can now use the Pointer tool to reshape the line as needed.

Editing shapes

- To move or resize the shape, select it with the Pointer tool and drag its bounding box. When resizing, use the **Shift** key if you wish to constrain the shape.

- Use **Flip Horizontal** and **Flip Vertical** on the Arrange menu (or right-click menu) to reorient directional shapes like arrows or callouts.

- You can deform an object and (optionally) its fill using the **Mesh Warp flyout** on the Tools toolbar (see **Applying a mesh warp envelope** on p. 67).

- You can adjust an object's crop outline using either the **Square** or **Irregular Crop** tool on the Tools toolbar, or crop a bottom shape to a top shape using **Tools>Crop to Shape**. (See **Cropping and combining objects** on p. 64.)

- You can convert any shape (such as **artistic text** or a **QuickShape**) to editable lines and nodes using **Convert to Curves** on the Tools menu.

- **Combining** joins two or more selected lines or drawn shapes (not QuickShapes) into a single group-like object, with a "hole" where the component objects' fills overlapped. You can apply formatting (such as line or fill) to the whole object and continue to edit individual nodes and segments with the Pointer tool.

- You can convert any shape into a **text frame** using **Convert to Shaped Frame** on the Tools menu.

- Use the **Weight** slider in the **Line tab** to change the weight (thickness) or type of the shape's border. Click one of the drop-down **Line** options to apply it.

- Use the **Swatches** tab to change the shape's line or fill colour (solid, gradient or bitmap). For details, see **Applying solid colours** or **Working with gradient and Bitmap fills** on p. 163 or 164, respectively.

- Use the **Opacity** tab to apply a gradient or Bitmap transparency effect. For details, see **Working with transparency** on p. 175.

To access all Line, Fill, and Transparency properties:

- Right-click on the shape and choose **Format>Line and Border...**, **Fill...**, or **Transparency....** The dialogs let you adjust all Line or Fill properties.

- You can also click the **Fill** or **Line/Border** button on the Tools toolbar's Fill flyout, or the **Transparency** button on the Transparency flyout.

Applying shadows, glow, bevel/emboss, colour fill

PagePlus provides a variety of **filter effects** that you can use to transform any object. **"3D"** filter effects let you create the impression of a textured surface. The **Colour Fill** effect applies a colour over any existing fill. Other filter effects are especially well adapted to text, as shown here:

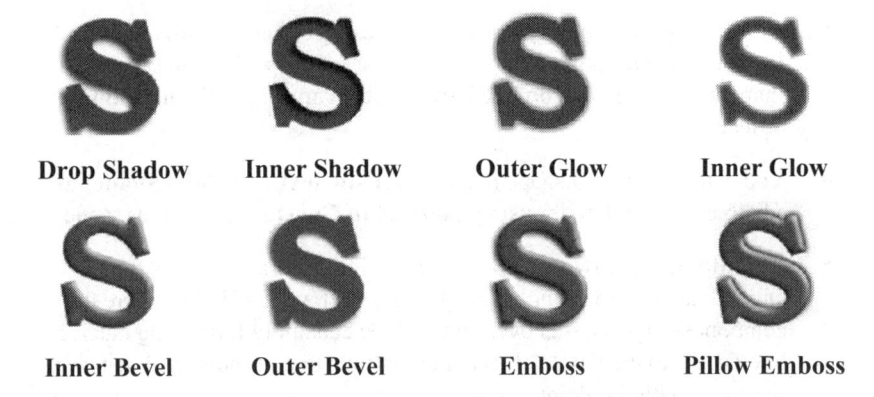

Drop Shadow   **Inner Shadow**   **Outer Glow**   **Inner Glow**

Inner Bevel   **Outer Bevel**   **Emboss**   **Pillow Emboss**

To apply a shadow, glow, bevel, or emboss filter effect:

1. Select an object and click the ![fx] **Filter Effects** button on the Attributes toolbar The Filter Effects dialog appears.

2. To apply a particular effect, check its box in the list at left. For certain effects, also select an effect type from the drop-down list. You can apply multiple effects to a given object.

3. For Shadow and Glow effects, choose a **blend mode** from the list. Click the **Colour** swatch to display the Adjust Colour dialog and change the base highlight or shadow colour from its default (either white or black)
OR
For Bevel and Emboss effects, choose a Highlight **blend mode** from the list and set the Opacity slider. Click the **Colour** swatch to display the Adjust Colour dialog and change the highlight colour from its default (white). Then choose a Shadow blend mode, opacity, and colour (default black).

4. To adjust the properties of a specific effect, select its name and vary the dialog controls. Adjust the sliders or enter specific values to vary the combined effect. (You can also select a slider and use the keyboard arrows.) Options differ from one effect to another.

5. Check the **Scale with Object** box if you want the effect to adjust in proportion to any change in the object's size. With the box unchecked, the effect's extent remains fixed if you resize the object.

6. Click **OK** to apply the effect to the selected object, or **Cancel** to abandon changes.

Colour Fill

The **Colour Fill** effect applies a colour over any existing fill, and lets you achieve some effects that are not possible with other controls. For example, you can use Colour Fill to force everything in a complex group to a single colour, or recolour a bitmap in a solid colour (effectively ignoring everything but the transparency).

Using 3D filter effects

3D filter effects create the impression of a textured surface on the object itself. You can use the **Filter Effects** dialog to apply one or more effects to the same object. Keep in mind is that none of these 3D effects will "do" anything to an unfilled object—you'll need to have a fill there to see the difference they make!

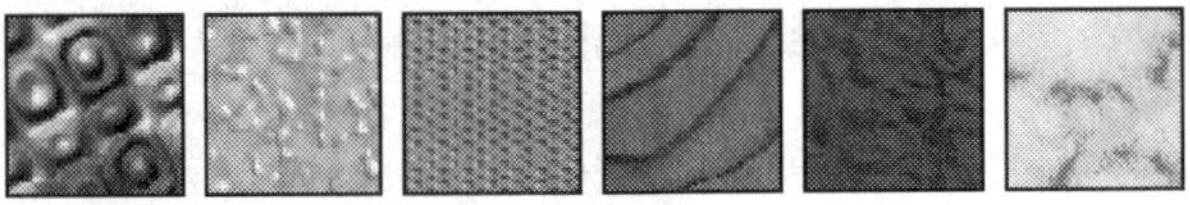

Overview

To apply a 3D filter effect to a selected object:

1. Click the *fx* **Filter Effects** button on the Attributes toolbar.
2. Check the **3D Effects** box at the left. The **3D Lighting** box is checked by default.

See below for details on each effect.

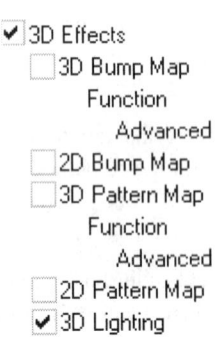

✔ 3D Effects
    ☐ 3D Bump Map
        Function
        Advanced
    ☐ 2D Bump Map
    ☐ 3D Pattern Map
        Function
        Advanced
    ☐ 2D Pattern Map
✔ 3D Lighting

3D Effects is a master switch for this group, and its settings of **Blur** and **Depth** make a great difference; you can click the "+" button to unlink them for independent adjustment.

3D Lighting provides a "light source" without which any depth information in the effect wouldn't be visible. The lighting settings let you illuminate your 3D landscape and vary its reflective properties.

You may wonder why all the 3D effects seem to have "map" in their name. The concept of a **map** is the key to understanding how these effects work: it means a channel of information overlaid on the image, storing values for each underlying fill pixel. You can think of the fill as a picture printed on a flexible sheet, which is flat to start with. Each 3D filter effect employs a map that interacts with the underlying fill to create the visual impression of a textured surface.

Bump Maps superimpose depth information for a bumpy, peak-and-valley effect. Using the flexible sheet metaphor, the bump map adds up-and-down contours and the object's fill "flexes" along with these bumps, like shrink-wrap, while a light from off to one side accentuates the contours.

Pattern Maps contribute colour variations using a choice of **blend modes** and opacity, for realistic (or otherworldly!) depictions of wood grain, marbling, and blotches or striations of all kinds.

Shape... + 3D Lighting + Bump Map + Pattern Map

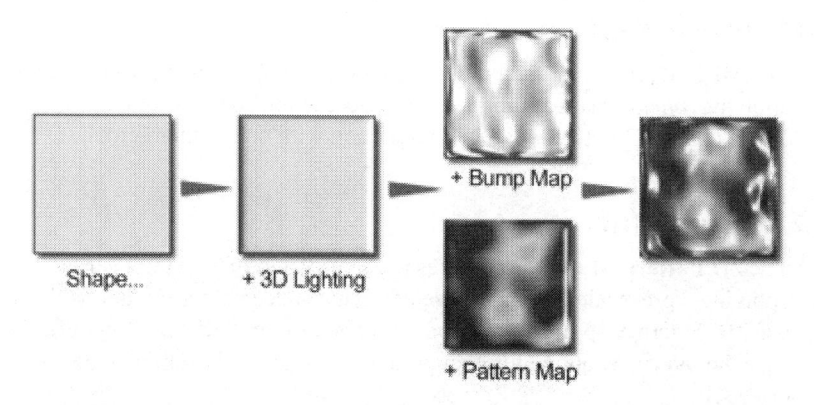

You'll notice that Bump Maps and Pattern Maps come in two varieties: "2D" and "3D." They are all three-dimensional effects—the 2D/3D distinction refers to how each one achieves its result. With the "2D map" variants, you begin by selecting a bitmap from a gallery. With the "3D" Bump Maps and Pattern Maps, you first pick a mathematical function. The function-based maps include data about the interior of the "space," while the bitmap-based maps describe only surface characteristics.

Multiple effects. You can combine multiple 3D filter effects, as in the illustration above. The effects are applied cumulatively, in a standard "pipeline" sequence: 3D Bump > 2D Bump > 3D Pattern > 2D Pattern > 3D Lighting.

The procedures for applying 3D Filter Effects are covered in the PagePlus Help but here's a quick review of each effect type.

3D Bump Map

The **3D Bump Map** effect creates the impression of a textured surface by applying a mathematical function you select to add depth information, for a peak-and-valley effect. You can use 3D Bump Map in conjunction with one or more additional 3D filter effects—but not with a 2D Bump Map.

2D Bump Map

The **2D Bump Map** effect creates the impression of a textured surface by applying a greyscale bitmap you select to add depth information, for a peak-and-valley effect. You can use 2D Bump Map in conjunction with one or more additional 3D filter effects—but not with a 3D Bump Map.

3D Pattern Map

The **3D Pattern Map** effect creates the impression of a textured surface by applying a mathematical function you select to introduce colour variations. You can use 3D Pattern Map in conjunction with one or more other 3D filter effects.

2D Pattern Map

The **2D Pattern Map** effect creates the impression of a textured surface by applying a greyscale bitmap you select to introduce colour variations. You can use 2D Pattern Map in conjunction with one or more other 3D filter effects. (See the **overview** above for background and technical details on these effects.)

3D Lighting

The **3D Lighting** effect works in conjunction with other 3D effects to let you vary the surface illumination and reflective properties.

Understanding blend modes

You can think of **blend modes** as different rules for putting pixels together to create a resulting colour. As applied in **filter effects**—including **shadows, glow, bevel, and emboss** as well as **Pattern Maps**—the blend mode is one of many settings that determine a colour change superimposed on the original object's pixels. Because the change is part of a filter effect, it doesn't actually alter the original pixel values. Note that blend modes work in relation to the colours of the object itself, and don't interact with background or underlying object colours. Changing the blend mode produces more dramatic results with some effects than with others (for example, with shadows they have negligible impact because the shadow is basically a blend with the background).

Here's a summary of available blend modes. In the following descriptions, "top colour" refers to the colour superimposed by the effect, while "bottom colour" refers to the colour prior to applying the effect.

- **Normal**
  The default blend mode. Blending of top colour and bottom colour pixels occurs only by varying the opacity setting. If the top colour's opacity setting is 100%, no blending occurs and only the top colour is visible.

- **Dissolve**
  Similar to Normal, but randomly selected top colour pixels are replaced with the bottom colour to create a speckled effect. The number of replaced pixels depends on the top colour's opacity (lower opacity, more replacements).

- **Multiply**
  The result is a combination of the top and bottom colour at each pixel position, always producing a darker value. Multiplying any colour with black yields black. Multiplying any colour with white leaves the colour unchanged. Successive multiplied paint strokes (other than black or white) produce a progressively darker "magic marker" effect.

- **Screen**
  Like Multiply, but the result is a combination of the inverse of the top and bottom colour at each pixel position, always producing a lighter value. Screening any colour with white yields white. Screening any colour with black leaves the colour unchanged. Successive screened paint strokes (other than black or white) produce a progressively lighter "bleaching" effect.

- **Overlay**
  Applies either Multiply or Screen, depending on the bottom colour at each pixel position. If the bottom is less than 50% grey, it multiplies; if greater, it screens. This tends to preserve highlights and shadows from the bottom along with main colours and patterns from the top. Compare to Hard Light.

- **Soft Light**
  Applies either Burn or Dodge, depending on the top colour at each pixel position. If the top is less than 50% grey, it burns; if greater, it dodges. This tends to add soft highlights and shadows to the image.

- **Hard Light**
  Applies either Multiply or Screen, depending on the top colour at each pixel position. If the top is less than 50% grey, it multiplies; if greater, it screens. This tends to add soft highlights and shadows to the image. Compare to Overlay.

- **Dodge**
  Lightens the image using lightness values of the top colour at each pixel position. Dodging with black has no effect.

- **Burn**
  Darkens the image using the lightness values of the top colour at each pixel position. Burning with white has no effect.

- **Lighten**
  The result is either the top or bottom colour at each pixel position, depending which is lighter. Darker colours are replaced.

- **Darken**
  The result is either the top or bottom colour at each pixel position, depending which is darker. Lighter colours are replaced.

- **Difference**
  The result is the difference between the top and bottom colour at each pixel position, with the same result no matter which colour is on top.

- **Exclusion**
  Similar to Difference, but a softer effect, with the same result no matter which colour is on top.

- **Hue**
  The result is a combination of the hue of the top colour with the lightness and saturation of the bottom colour.

- **Saturation**
  The result is a combination of the saturation of the top colour with the hue and lightness of the bottom colour. No change over greyscale (0% saturation) regions.

- **Colour**
  The result is a combination of the hue and saturation of the top colour with the lightness of the bottom colour. Because lightness values (greyscale levels) are preserved, this mode is useful for tinting greyscale images. Compare Lightness.

Each of the above blend modes is supported with an example in the PagePlus Help.

Feathering

Feathering is a filter effect that adds a soft or blurry edge to any object. It's great for blending single objects into a composition, vignetted borders on photos, and much more. You can apply feathering in conjunction with other filter effects.

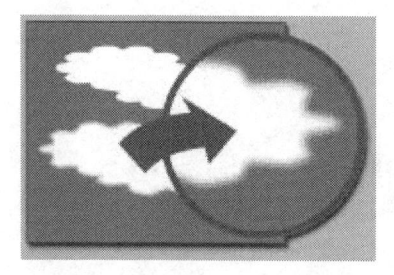

To apply feathering:

1. Select an object and choose **Filter Effects...** from the Format menu, or right-click the object and choose **Filter Effects....** The Filter Effects dialog appears.
2. Check the **Feathering** box at left.
3. Adjust the sliders or enter specific values to vary the feathering effect. (You can also select a slider and use the keyboard arrows.)
   • **Opacity** (0 to 100%) controls the opacity of shadow pixels.
   • **Blur** controls the "fuzziness" of the edge.
4. Check the **Scale with Object** box if you want the effect to adjust in proportion to any change in the object's size. With the box unchecked, the effect's extent remains fixed if you resize the object.
5. Click **OK** to apply the effect to the selected object, or **Cancel** to abandon changes.

Adding dimensionality (Instant 3D)

Using the **Instant 3D** feature, you can easily transform flat shapes and text into three-dimensional objects with precise control over settings like extrusion, rotation, lighting, and texture. The underlying base object remains editable.

To add dimensionality:

1. Select an object and click the [icon] **Instant 3D** button on the Attributes toolbar (or choose **Instant 3D...** from the Format menu).
2. The Instant 3D dialog appears, with the **3D Effects** box checked at the left. (To switch off dimensionality once it's been applied to an object, simply uncheck the box.)
3. Change your 3D effect options for Extrusion, Lens, X Rotation, Y Rotation, and Z Rotation.
4. The other settings for Bevel, Light, Texture, and Render can be applied—all the settings together contribute to the 3D effect applied to the selected object. Click a category in the list at left and vary the dialog controls. See the PagePlus Help for more details.
5. Click **OK** when you've made your choices.

To edit base properties of a 3D object:

- Select the 3D object, then click its Edit button, i.e.

Adding borders

A **border** in PagePlus is a repeating, decorative element that can be set to enclose an object. Borders work especially well with imported pictures.

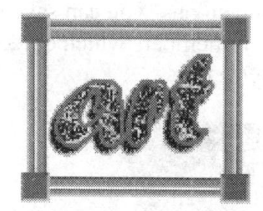

To add a border to an object:

1. Click the ![] **Line/Border** button on the Tools toolbar's Fill flyout.
2. If you want to apply the border to specific edges of the object, use the **Border Edges** tab.
   - To select **all edges** or **no edges**, click the corresponding icon the top row.
   - To toggle a single edge, click the corresponding icon in the bottom row. The preview at the left indicates with bolding which edges of the selected object's border will be updated with the current Border tab settings when you click **OK**.
3. To define the border, select the **Border** tab. In the Side list, select a border preset. You can use the up/down arrows to move through the list, and preview each border in the window at the right. To remove a border, select "None".
4. To keep the corner pattern the same as the side, leave **Keep side and corners the same** checked. To mix and match, uncheck the box and select a preset from the Corner list.
5. Choose an Alignment setting to fit the border to the **Outside** or **Inside** of the object, or straddling the **Middle** of its bounding box.
6. Set other properties as needed:
   - To vary the border width, select or type a value in the Weight list.
   - If **Behind contents** is checked, the inner half of the border extends behind the object. If unchecked, the whole border appears in front (the wider the border, the more it encroaches on the filled region).
   - If **Scale with object** is checked, both border and object change together if you resize the object. If unchecked, the border weight remains constant during resizing.
7. Click **OK** when you're done.

Using object styles

Object styles benefit your design efforts in much the same way as **text styles** and **colour schemes**. Once you've come up with a set of attributes that you like—properties like line colour, fill, border, and so on—you can save this cluster of attributes as a named style. PagePlus remembers which objects are using that style, and the style appears in the Styles tab.

Here's how object styles work to your advantage:

- Any time you want to alter some aspect of the style (for example, change the line colour), you simply change the style definition. Instantly, all objects in your publication sharing that style update accordingly.

- Object styles you've saved globally appear not only in the original publication but in any new publication, so you can reuse exactly the same attractive combination of attributes for any subsequent design effort.

As a bonus, the Styles tab ships with multiple galleries of predesigned styles that you can apply to any object, or customise to suit your own taste!

Each object style can include settings for a host of object attributes, such as **line colour**, **line style**, **fill**, **transparency**, **filter effects**, **font**, and **border**. The freedom to include or exclude certain attributes, and the nearly unlimited range of choices for each attribute, makes this a powerful tool in the designer's arsenal.

To apply an object style to one or more objects:

1. Display the **Styles** tab.
2. Expand the drop-down menu to display a tree-structure menu showing 3D, Filter effect and Materials categories. Navigate the menu to select a category while previewing available styles as thumbnails in the lower panel.
3. Click a style thumbnail in the panel to apply it to the selected object(s). Drag and drop the thumbnail onto any object.

To create a new object style based on an existing object's attributes:

1. Right-click the object and choose **Format>Object Style>Create**.

The Style Attributes Editor dialog appears, with a tree listing object attributes on the left and a preview region on the right.

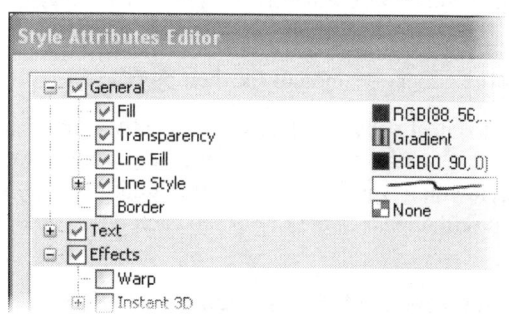

2. Click to expand or collapse sections within the attributes tree. Check any attributes you want to include in the style definition, and uncheck any you don't want to include.

3. If you want to change any of the current object settings, double-click an attribute (or select it and click the **Edit** button). This will bring up a detailed dialog for the particular attribute.

4. The **Object** pane in the preview region shows the currently selected object after applying the defined style. Select the **Artistic Text** or **Frame Text** tab to see the style applied to sample objects of those types.

5. Click the **Browse...** button to select the gallery category where you want to locate the style thumbnail.

6. Type a name to identify the gallery thumbnail.

7. Click **OK**. A thumbnail for the new object style appears in the designated gallery.

Once an object style is listed in a gallery, you can modify it or create a copy (for example, to define a derivative style) by clicking the bottom right-hand corner of its gallery thumbnail and choosing **Edit....**

To remove an object style from a gallery:

- Click the bottom corner thumbnail and choose **Delete** from the drop-down menu.

To unlink an object from its style definition:

- Right-click the object and choose **Format>Object Style>Unlink**.

If you've applied a style to an object but have lost track of the thumbnail—or want to confirm which style is actually being used on an object—you can quickly locate the thumbnail from the object.

To locate an object's style in the Styles tab:

- Right-click the object and choose **Format>Object Style>Locate in Studio**.

The Styles tab displays the gallery thumbnail for the object's style.

Normally, a publication's object styles are just stored locally—that is, as part of that publication; they don't automatically carry over to new publications. If you've created a new style you'll want to use in another publication, you can save it globally so that it will appear in the Styles tab each time you open a new publication.

To save a publication's object styles globally:

- Choose **Save Object Styles** from the Tools menu.

Using Colours and Fills

7

Applying solid colours

PagePlus offers a number of ways to apply solid colours to objects of different kinds:

- You can apply solid colours to an object's **line** or **fill**. As you might expect, QuickShapes and closed shapes (see **Drawing and editing shapes** on p. 145) have both line and fill properties, whereas straight and freehand lines have only a line property.

- Characters in text objects can have fill colour or highlight colour, and text frames and table cells can have a background fill independent of the characters they contain.

- You can colourise a paint-type (bitmap) picture—that is, recolour it to use a different colour. If you recolour a full-colour picture, the colours will convert to tints or shades of the specified colour. You can also apply tinting to a full-colour picture to produce a low-intensity picture (useful for backgrounds behind text).

You can use the Colour tab, Swatches tab or a dialog box to apply solid colours to an object.

To apply a solid colour via the Colour tab:

1. Select the object(s) or highlight a range of text.
2. Click the **Colour** tab from which you can apply colour from one of several colour pallettes.
3. Click the **Fill**, **Line**, or **Text** button at the top of the tab to determine where colour will be applied. The colour of the underline reflects the colour of your selected object.
4. Select a colour from the colour spectrum or sliders.

To apply a solid colour via the Swatches tab:

1. Select the object(s) or highlight a range of text.
2. Click the **Swatches** tab.
3. Click the **Fill**, **Line**, or **Text** button at the top of the tab to determine where colour will be applied.
4. Select a colour sample from the Publication palette (colours previously applied to your publication) or Standard palette (supplied preset swatches).

Use **Format>Fill...** to apply colour via a dialog.

164 | Using Colours and Fills PagePlus 11 User Guide

- To load a specific palette (such as **Standard CMYK** or **Standard RGB**), choose Palettes from the Tools menu and select palette's name submenu. For more details, see **Managing publication colours and palettes** on p. 172.

- The top left cell in the colour spectrum (Colour tab) or palette samples (Swatches tab) shows ▨, which represents either None (a transparent interior for objects with line/fill properties) or Original (for pictures only, to reset the object to its original colours).

Working with gradient and Bitmap fills

Gradient fills provide a gradation or spectrum of colours spreading between two or more colours. A gradient fill has an editable path with nodes that mark the origin of each of these key colours. A Bitmap fill uses a named bitmap—often a material, pattern, or background image—to fill an object. PagePlus supplies over 200 preset gradient or Bitmap fills on the Swatches tab, and you can import your own. You can recolour Bitmap fills using the "Colour Fill" **filter effect.**

Linear   Ellipse   Conical   Bitmap

You can apply gradient and Bitmap fills from the Swatches tab to **shapes**, **text frames**, **table cells**, and to the actual characters in **artistic text** objects. Using the **Fill** tool from the Attributes toolbar, you can vary the fill's path on an object for different effects.

Applying different transparency effects (using the **Opacity** tab) won't alter the object's fill settings as such, but may significantly alter a fill's actual appearance.

Applying a gradient or Bitmap fill

There are several ways to apply a gradient or Bitmap fill: using the Fill tool, the **Swatches** tab, or a dialog. The dialog lets you add or subtract **key colours** from the gradient (see **Editing the gradient fill spectrum** on p. 167), apply different key colours to individual nodes, or vary the overall shading of the effect applied to the object.

To apply a gradient fill with the Fill tool:

1. Select an object.
2. Click the **Fill Tool** button on the Attributes toolbar.
3. Click and drag on the object to define the fill path. The object takes a simple Linear fill, grading from the object's current colour to white.

To apply a gradient or Bitmap fill using the Swatches tab:

1. Click the Swatches tab and ensure the **Fill** button is selected. The colour of the underline reflects the colour of your selected object.
2. For gradient fills, select Linear, Ellipse or Conical as the gradient type from the **Gradient** button's drop-down menu.
   OR

   For bitmap fills, select a drop-down menu category from the **Bitmap** button.
3. Select the object(s), and click the appropriate gallery swatch for the fill you want to apply.
   OR
   Drag from the gallery swatch onto any object and release the mouse button.
4. If needed, adjust the fill's **Tint** at the bottom of the tab with the tab slider or set a percentage value in the input box.

To apply or edit a gradient or Bitmap fill using a dialog:

1. Right-click the object and choose **Format>Fill...**, or select it and choose **Fill...** from the Format menu.
2. Choose the fill type and the desired fill category. Note that you can also use the dialog to apply a solid fill, or no fill.
3. For a two-colour gradient, click the **From** button to pick a starting colour, and click the **To** button to pick an ending colour. A two-colour gradient has two nodes, one at each end of its path. For Bitmap fills, select "Bitmap" from the **Type** drop-down menu, choose a category and click a gallery sample.
4. For gradient fills, click the **Edit** button if you want to add or subtract key colours from the gradient (see **Editing the fill spectrum** on p. 167), apply different key colours to individual nodes, or vary the overall shading of the effect. You can adjust the fill's shade/tint as needed using the list.
5. Click **OK** to apply the effect of the fill to the object.

Editing the fill path

When you select a fillable object, the Fill tool becomes available (otherwise it's greyed out). If the object uses a **gradient fill**, you'll see the **fill path** displayed as a line, with nodes marking where the spectrum between each key colour begins and ends. Adjusting the node positions determines the actual spread of colours between nodes. You can also edit a gradient fill by adding, deleting, or changing key colours (see below).

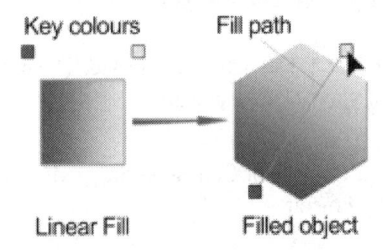

To adjust the gradient fill path on a selected object:

1. Click the ![] **Fill Tool** button on the Attributes toolbar. The object's fill path appears.

2. Use the Fill tool to drag the start and end path nodes, or click on the object for a new start node and drag out a new fill path. The gradient starts where you place the start node, and ends where you place the end node.

Each gradient fill type has a characteristic path. For example, Linear fills have single-line paths, while Radial fills have a two-line path so you can adjust the fill's extent in two directions away from the centre. If the object uses a **Bitmap fill**, you'll see the fill path displayed as two lines joined at a centre point. Nodes mark the fill's centre and edges.

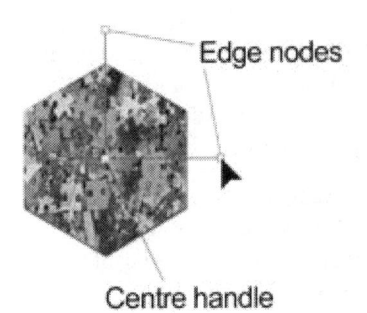

Unlike the other fill types, Bitmap fills don't simply "end" at the edges of their fill path. Rather, they tile (repeat) so you can fill indefinitely large regions at any scale. By dragging the edge nodes in or out with the Fill tool, you can "zoom" in or out on the fill pattern.

For example, these two shapes use identical Bitmap fills with different fill path settings:

Nodes far away   Nodes near

To adjust the path of a Bitmap fill on a selected object:

1. Click the ⬨ **Fill Tool** button on the Attributes toolbar. The object's fill path appears.
2. Use the Fill tool to drag the centre and/or edge nodes, or click on the object for a new centre node and drag out a new fill path.
3. To reposition the fill's centre, drag the centre node.
4. To adjust the fill's extent and tiling, drag one or both edge nodes in or out with respect to the centre.
5. To create a skewed or tilted fill region, drag one or both edge nodes sideways.
6. To tilt the fill path in 15-degree increments, hold down the **Shift** key while dragging. The fill path is unskewed and "regularly sized"—that is, its size jumps in steps. To preserve the fill's aspect ratio, hold down the **Ctrl** key. For a combined effect, use both keys together.

> TIP: The **Ctrl**-constrain technique is convenient if you want a Bitmap fill to extend to fill a box without tiling. One of the "regular" steps includes a setting where the fill matches the object's bounding box.

Editing the gradient fill spectrum

Whether you're editing a gradient fill that's been already been applied to an object, or redefining one of the gallery fills, the basic concepts are the same. Whereas solid fills use a single colour, all gradient fills utilise at least two **key colours**, with a spread of hues in between each key colour, creating a "spectrum" effect. You can either edit the fill spectrum directly, using the Fill tool in conjunction with the Schemes tab, or use a dialog.

The editing of gradient fills is a complex operation and is covered in full detail in the PagePlus Help.

Changing the set of gradient gallery fills

If you've defined a new gradient fill by setting fill path and/or key colours, you can add it to the set of gradient gallery fills shown on the Swatches tab so that it will be available to use again. You can also add new fills or delete any of the existing gallery fills.

To add an object's fill to a fill gallery:

- Right-click the object and choose **Format>Add Fill to Studio**. The fill is added to the gradient fill gallery of the Swatches tab.

To define a new gallery fill:

1. Right-click any gallery sample and choose **Add...**.
2. Use the Object Fill dialog to create your new gradient fill.
3. Click **OK** to accept changes, or **Cancel** to abandon changes.

To delete a gallery fill:

- Right-click its sample and choose **Delete**.

Deleting a gallery fill doesn't affect any objects that have already been given that fill.

Changing the set of Bitmap gallery fills

The Bitmap gallery on the Swatches tab provides a large selection of bitmaps, grouped into categories like Abstract, Material, Patterns, and so on. You can add or delete a bitmap or an entire category.

To add a category to the Bitmap fill gallery:

1. Right-click any thumbnail and choose **Add Category...**.
2. Type a category name into the dialog, and click **OK**. A new empty gallery category appears.

To delete a category from the Bitmap fill gallery:

1. Choose the category to delete in the drop-down list.
2. Right-click any thumbnail and choose **Delete Category...**.

To delete a Bitmap fill from the gallery:

- Right-click the thumbnail and choose **Delete**. Click **Yes** to confirm deletion.

Deleting a gallery fill doesn't affect any objects that have already been given that fill.

To import a bitmap image file to the Bitmap fill gallery:

1. Choose the category to which you want to add a bitmap.
2. Right-click any thumbnail and choose **Add**.... The standard Import Picture dialog appears.
3. Use the dialog to locate the bitmap image file to import, and click **Open**.

A bitmap thumbnail appears, labelled with the image file name, in the selected gallery.

Setting the default fill

The **default fill** means the fill that will be applied to the next new object you create.

To set local defaults for a particular type of object:

1. Create a single sample object and fine-tune its properties as desired—or use an existing object that already has the right properties. (For QuickShapes, you can use any QuickShape; all share the same set of defaults.)
2. Select the object that's the basis for the new defaults and choose **Update Object Default** from the Format menu.

Using colour schemes

A **colour scheme** in PagePlus is a cluster of five complementary colours that you can apply to specific elements in one or more publications. The **Schemes** tab displays over 80 preset schemes which can be selected at any point during the design process. Each publication can have just one colour scheme at a time; the current scheme is highlighted in the **Schemes** tab. You can easily switch schemes, modify scheme colours, apply schemes to any publication, even create your own custom schemes. Colour schemes are saved globally, so the full set of schemes is always available.

To select a colour scheme:

1. Go to the **Schemes** tab which shows the currently assigned scheme highlighted in the list.
2. Click a different colour scheme sample. Any regions in the publication that have been assigned one of the five colour scheme numbers (see below) are updated with the corresponding colour from the new scheme.

You can repeat this selection process indefinitely. When you save a publication, its current colour scheme is saved along with the document.

How colour schemes work

Colour schemes in PagePlus work much like a paint-by-numbers system, where various regions of a layout are coded with numbers, and a specific colour is assigned (by number) to each region. For example, imagine a line drawing coded with the numbers 1 through 5. To fill it in, you'd use paint from jars also numbered 1 through 5. Swapping different colours into the paint jars, while keeping the numbers on the drawing the same, would produce quite a different painting.

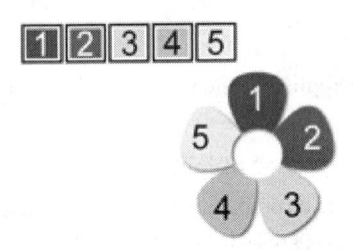

In PagePlus, the "paint jars" are five numbers you can assign to objects in your publication. They're known as "Scheme Colour 1," "Scheme Colour 2," and so on. When you apply Scheme Colour 1 to an object, it's like saying, "Put the colour from jar number 1 here."

- The **Schemes** tab shows the various available schemes, each with a different set of five colours in the five "jars." Whichever named colour scheme you select, that scheme's first colour (as shown in its sample) will appear in regions defined as Scheme Colour 1, its second colour will map to Scheme Colour 2, and so on throughout the publication.

The example below shows three different schemes as applied to a design that's been marked with Scheme Colours 1 through 5 as in the example above.

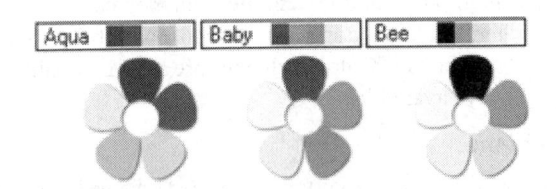

Applying scheme colours to objects

If you create new elements in a Page Wizard publication, or start a publication from scratch, how can you extend a colour scheme to the new objects? Although you'll need to spend some time working out which colour combinations look best, the mechanics of the process are simple. Recalling the paint-by-numbers example above, all you need to do is assign one of the five scheme colour numbers to an object's line and/or fill.

To assign a scheme colour to an object:

1. Display the **Swatches** tab. The five colours in the current scheme appear as numbered samples at the bottom left-hand corner of the tab. (In Web mode, you'll also see additional samples labelled **H**, **F**, and **B**, which apply to hyperlink and background colours as detailed in **Choosing Web site colours**.)

2. Select the object and choose a ▬ **Fill**, ▬ **Line**, or **A** **Text** button at the top of the tab depending on the desired effect.

3. Click on a scheme colour that you want to apply to the fill, line and text (or you can drag the colour instead).

4. If an object's fill uses a scheme colour, the corresponding sample will be highlighted whenever the object is selected.

Modifying and creating colour schemes

If you've tried various colour schemes but haven't found one that's quite right, you can modify any of the colours in an existing scheme to create a new one, or create your own named scheme from scratch.

To modify or create a colour scheme:

1. Select any colour scheme sample in the **Schemes** tab, click on the ▷ **Options** button and choose **Scheme Manager** from the drop-down menu. The **Scheme Manager** dialog appears, with the current scheme colours shown on the Edit tab.

2. To select a different scheme, switch to the dialog's **Schemes** tab and select a scheme in the scrolling list. Clicking **OK** at this point applies the scheme to the publication, or you can go back to the Edit tab and adjust scheme colours.

3. On the Edit tab, each of the five scheme colour numbers (plus the Hyperlink, Followed Hyperlink, and background Page Colour if in Web mode) has its own drop-down list, showing available colours in the PagePlus palette.

4. To set or change a scheme colour or adjunct colour, simply click the adjacent button and select a new colour. Click **More Colours...** to display the Colour Selector.

5. To store the modified scheme in the Schemes tab, click **Save Scheme....** If modifying an existing scheme, leave the name unaltered. If creating a new scheme, enter a new name.

6. To apply the scheme to the current publication (or web site), click **OK**.

Managing publication colours and palettes

Each PagePlus publication has a particular set of colours, known as a **palette**, which appear as a set of gallery swatches in the **Swatches** tab. PagePlus ships with over 10 standard palettes, stored separately as files with the .PLT file extension (e.g., RGB.plt). New paper and Web publications initially use the standard RGB palette (you can change the default palette if you wish).

Any new colours you create will automatically be added to the **Swatches** tab (in the **Publication palette**, which hosts other colours previously used in the current publication along with a selection of commonly used colours (e.g., Red, Green, Blue, etc.). Added colours are loaded back into the gallery when you reopen the publication. However, a publication can also include colours that aren't part of its palette, and hence don't appear in the Swatches tab. For example, you might apply a gallery colour to an object and then modify its shade/tint value, creating a unique colour. Any such colours are of course saved in the publication, but they remain separate from the palette itself unless you explicitly add them.

PagePlus lets you quickly load standard RGB, CMYK or "themed" palettes as well as save and load custom palettes for use in other publications.

Normally, the Publication palette (as shown in the Swatches tab) is just saved locally, along with the publication's current defaults. That is, the colours don't automatically carry over to new publications. If you've added new colours to this palette and will want to use them in other publications, you can either (1) save the palette as described below, and then load it as needed into another publication; or (2) use the Save Defaults command to record the current palette globally, so it (rather than the original standard palette) will be loaded whenever you create a new publication. For details, see **Updating and saving defaults** on p. 46.

To add a custom colour to the Publication palette automatically:

- With the Colour tab selected, pick a colour from the displayed colour spectrum.

OR:

- Use the **Colour Picker** on the Colour tab to select any colour already on your page. Remember to hold down the button and drag the cursor onto the page.

> If you don't want to add colours automatically, uncheck **Automatically Add to Publication palette** on the Colour tab's option button.

You can also add colours to the Publication palette by right-clicking on any sample in your Publication palette then selecting the **Add** option, or by using the Palette Manager (see below).

To add an object's solid fill colour to the Publication palette:

- Right-click the object and choose **Format>Add Fill to Studio**. The colour is added to the Publication palette of the Swatches tab directly.

To edit a specific palette colour in the Publication palette:

1. Right-click a sample in the Publication palette of the Swatches tab and choose **Edit**.
2. Choose a different colour from the colour spectrum in the **Colour Selector** dialog.
3. Click the **OK** button. The colour is updated in the Publication palette.

> NOTE: Colours present in the standard or "themed" palettes can be edited once added to the Publication palette as above.

To remove a colour from the Publication palette:

- Right-click on the colour in the Publication palette of the Swatches tab and choose **Delete**. Alternatively, use the Palette Manager.

To load a named palette:

1. In the Swatches tab, click the down arrow on the **Palette** button.
2. From the resulting drop-down menu, select a standard (e.g., standard cmyk or rgb) or "themed" palette.

The loaded palette's colours appear as swatches in the **Swatches** tab, replacing the swatches previously visible.

Using the Colour Selector and Palette Manager

The Palette Manager and Colour Selector are complementary dialogs to the Colour and Swatches tabs.

- The **Colour Selector** lets you choose a colour to apply or mix custom colours. Its **Models** tab displays the colour space of several established colour models: RGB (red, green blue), HSL (hue, saturation, luminosity), CMYK (cyan, magenta, yellow, black), and PANTONE® Colours at the same time. For all colour models, the values are in the range of 0 to 255. Its **Publication palette** tab lets you modify the set of colours associated with the current publication.

- The **Palette Manager** extends the Colour Selector's Publication palette tab. It not only lets you modify the publication's current palette but also load and save named palettes.

To display the Palette Manager:

- Choose **Palettes** from the Tools menu, then choose **Palette Manager...** from the submenu.

To add a PANTONE® colour to the Publication palette:

- Display the Palette Manager, select **New**, then in the Model list on the **Models** tab choose **PANTONE® Colours**.

PANTONE refers to Pantone, Inc.'s check-standard trademark for colour reproduction and colour reproduction materials. For details, see **Colour matching with PANTONE® or Serif colours** on p. 179.

To save the Publication palette:

- In the Palette Manager, click **Save As...** and specify a name for the palette.

The saved palette's name will appear in the drop-down menu of the **Palette** button (Swatches tab).

> NOTE: Another option if you'll want to use the current palette in another publication is to use the Save Defaults command to record the colour settings globally, so they will be available whenever you create a new publication. For details, see **Updating and saving defaults** on p. 46.

Working with transparency

Transparency effects are great for highlights, shading and shadows, and simulating "rendered" realism. They can make the critical difference between flat-looking illustrations and images with depth and snap. PagePlus fully supports variable transparency and lets you apply gradient or Bitmap transparencies to create your own 32-bit, anti-aliased images. You can export transparent graphics as GIFs, PNGs, or TIFs and preserve transparency effects in both your printed output and your Web pages.

In the illustration below, the pentagonal shape has had a Linear transparency applied, with more transparency at the lower end of the path and less at the upper end. It makes a difference which object is in front (here, the pentagon); where there's more transparency, more of the object(s) behind will show through.

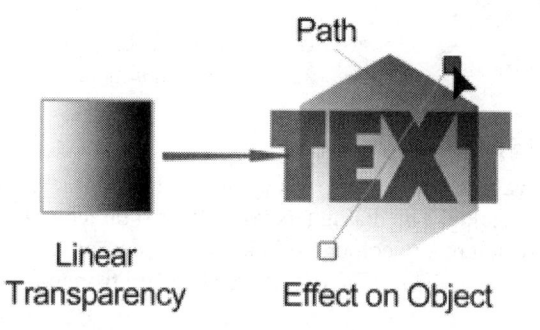

Linear Transparency — Effect on Object

The concept of transparency

Transparency may seem a bit tricky because by definition, you can't "see" it the way you can see a colour fill applied to an object. In fact, it's there all the time in PagePlus. Each new object has a transparency property: the default just happens to be None—that is, no transparency.

Varying the transparency of an object gives the effect of variable erasure, but it leaves the original object intact—you can always remove or alter the transparency later. Transparencies work rather like fills that use "disappearing ink" instead of colour. A gradient transparency varies from more "disappearing" to less, as in the illustration above.

In PagePlus, the available transparency effects are all comparable to greyscale fills of the same name, and most transparency effects have a path you can edit—in this case, with the Transparency tool.

Transparency gallery samples in the **Opacity tab** show gradations from light to dark, with the lighter portions representing more transparency. Any sample can be edited to create a new gallery sample, or a new transparency can be added or deleted to the tab.

- **Solid** transparency distributes the transparency evenly across the object.
- **Linear**, **Radial**, and **Conical** transparencies provide a simple gradient effect, with a range from clear to opaque. (To review the concept, see **Working with gradient and Bitmap fills** on p. 164).
- The **Bitmap** drop-down menu in the Swatches tab hosts texture maps under a series of categories, including a special category of "Photo Edge Effects" for soft-edge masking.
- At left, a Photo Edge Transparency (with skewed path) on a metafile.

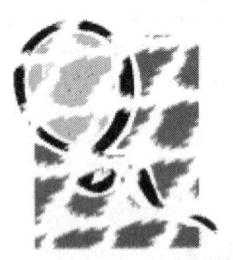

Applying transparency

There are three ways to apply transparency: using the Transparency tool, the **Opacity** tab, or a dialog. The dialog lets you add or subtract nodes from the gradient, apply different key colours to individual nodes, or vary the overall shading of the effect applied to the object (see **Editing transparency effects** on p. 177).

To apply a transparency effect with the Transparency tool:

1. Select an object.
2. Click the **Transparency Tool** button on the Attributes toolbar.
3. Click and drag on the object to define the transparency path. The object takes a simple Linear transparency, grading from opaque to clear.

To apply a transparency effect using the Opacity tab:

1. Go to the **Opacity** tab. You'll see the Transparency gallery, displaying available transparency samples. The lighter portions of the samples represent more transparency.
2. Select the object(s) and click a gallery sample for the transparency you want to apply.

To apply or edit a transparency using a dialog:

1. Click the **Transparency** button on the Attributes toolbar's Transparency flyout.
2. Choose the desired type of fill. In addition:
   - For a Bitmap fill, select a desired bitmap transparency category and click a thumbnail.
   - For a gradient effect, whether the fill is a Linear, Ellipse or Conical.
   - For a simple gradient with two nodes—one at each end of its path—click the **From** button to pick a starting opacity value, and click the **To** button to pick an ending value.
   - Click the **Edit** button if you want to add or subtract nodes from the gradient (see "Varying a gradient fill" below), or apply different values to individual nodes.
3. Click **OK** to apply the transparency effect to the object.

Editing transparency effects

Once you've applied a transparency, you can adjust its **path** on the object with the **Transparency Tool** button.

By clicking the **Transparency** button, the level of solid transparency can be adjusted with the Level slider on the Transparency dialog. Likewise, for gradient fills (but not Bitmap fills), you can adjust the **level** of transparency along the path by altering the opacity values of any selected node present on the path—this can be done directly or via the **Transparency** dialog. **Simple** gradient transparency effects have only two nodes, one at each end of the path. **Multi-level** gradient transparency effects include extra nodes along the gradient path.

Adding a level of transparency means varying the transparency gradient by introducing a new node and assigning it a greyscale value. For gradient transparencies with multiple nodes, each node has its own level, comparable to a key colour in a gradient fill. You can alter the levels of gradient transparency for any nodes (not those of Bitmap transparencies) to vary the transparency effect.

Effect on Object

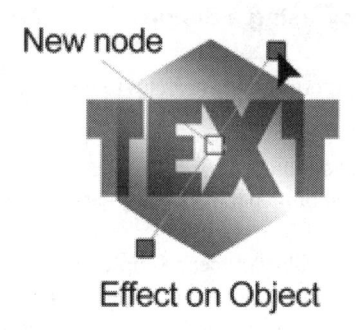

Changing the set of gallery transparencies

If you've defined a new gradient transparency by setting path and/or level, you can add it to the set of gallery transparencies shown on the Opacity tab so that it will be available to use again. You can also edit or delete any of the gallery transparencies.

To add an object's transparency to the gallery:

- Right-click the object and choose **Format>Add Transparency to Studio**. The transparency setting is stored as a new sample in the Opacity tab.

To edit a gallery transparency:

1. Right-click a sample and choose **Edit**.
2. In the Transparency dialog, choose a new level of transparency with the slider or input box.
3. Click **OK**. The new sample is shown at the end of the samples shown in the Opacity tab.

To delete a gallery transparency:

- Right-click the sample and choose **Delete**.

Deleting a gallery transparency doesn't affect any objects that have already been given that effect.

Setting the default transparency

The **default transparency** means the transparency that will be applied to the next new object you create.

For information on setting defaults in PagePlus, see **Updating and saving defaults** on p. 46.

Colour Matching with Pantone or Serif Colours

When it comes to colour reproduction, printing devices and computer screens are on totally different "wavelengths."

Printing creates colours by mixing inks which absorb light. Mix the four CMYK **process inks** (Cyan, Magenta, Yellow, and blacK), and you get black. No ink gives you white (i.e., the colour of the paper)—so if you want white, you must use no ink! CMYK is a **subtractive** model: the more ink applied, the less light reflected, hence the darker the colour.

A monitor produces an image by mixing light using the three primary colours—Red, Green and Blue—hence, RGB. RGB is an **additive** model. Mix all three colours together and you get white light. Turn all the elements off and you get black. Different brightnesses of each element give the typical computer monitor a range or **gamut** of colours much greater than can be printed with CMYK inks.

The fundamental difference between the CMYK and RGB colour models, and the limited gamut of the printed page compared to the computer screen, create the **colour matching** problem: the challenge of getting your printed output to match what you see in your on-screen publication layout. By calibrating your equipment and using great care, you can achieve a close approximation—but the cardinal rule is "Trust, but verify!" Never simply assume the colours on your screen will turn out exactly the same when printed. It's just very difficult to convert accurately between the two models!

For accurate colour reproduction, use the Serif *Colour Chart*, available separately. The chart includes over 350 standard CMYK colours printed on two different finishes of paper. Pick the colours you like from the paper swatches and then use only those colours as you design your publication. When you've started with a New Publication, the Swatches tab displays a set of colours identical to those on the Serif Colour Chart—select "standard cmyk" from the Palette button's drop-down menu to view them. Use these colours and standard CMYK colours for printing, and you're guaranteed a match between the chart samples and your finished piece!

Another solution is to use the PANTONE® Colour Picker, built into PagePlus, which lets you add PANTONE colours to the colour palette. The PANTONE Colour Matching system is an internationally recognised system for colour matching. When a PANTONE colour is output, PagePlus uses optimised colour values to achieve a better colour match. The on-screen colour display is only an approximation—don't rely on it for accurate colour matching. For precise reproduction, use official PANTONE colour reference materials (swatches).

The International Colour Consortium (ICC) defines industry standards for converting colour information between various colour spaces and gamuts. For more accurate results, we strongly recommend that you take advantage of PagePlus 10's colour management features, which let you select ICC device profiles that specify how the internal RGB and/or CMYK colours in your publication's fills and bitmaps will map to on-screen and printed colours. Choose **Colour Management...** from the Tools menu to view a dialog that lets you select from profiles available on your system. Your monitor or printer manufacturer's Web site should have additional information on how those devices use ICC profiles. Another good source is **www.color.org**.

A good rule of thumb, if you're especially concerned about colour accuracy, is to produce a Cromalin, Matchprint, or other press proof prior to running the print job. It won't exactly match your final printed page, but will perform a final check that the colours are OK at the prepress stage. Don't authorise the print run until you're happy with your colours as seen in the proof!

Managing Screen and Output Colours

Regardless of the level of colour management you implement, accurate **colour calibration** of your monitor is important. And if you're trying to visually match onscreen colours to a printed page, it's critical. Note that after successful calibration, monitor colours will appear less vibrant as they will be restricted to the gamut of colours that printed inks can achieve.

All computer monitors needs RGB data to display onscreen. However, one monitor's interpretation of RGB green might be different from another's. **Colour profiles** exist to iron out the differences. PagePlus supports a colour profile called **sRGB**. If you set your monitor to its sRGB mode (check the manufacturer's instructions), you can be assured that PagePlus is displaying colours as realistically as possible. Some monitors have their own colour profile instead. PagePlus lets you load a specific monitor's profile (see PagePlus help), again ensuring accurate colour display. Be sure to choose a colour palette (CMYK or RGB) as described above to match the type of output you're aiming for.

Another approach favoured by professionals is to employ specialized hardware or software to verify that screen colours match established standards. Check the Web for products and advice.

For many non-professionals, a common-sense approach and a few adjustments will help to prevent disastrous mismatches between onscreen and printed work. Here are a few things to keep in mind:

- **Ambient lighting**
 The type and quality of background lighting at your workspace can seriously affect your perception of colours displayed on the monitor. The same monitor display can appear very different under fluorescent lighting, which has a bluish tinge, than under warmer, redder incandescent lighting. Daylight itself is quite variable over the course of a day or even a few moments. Ideally you should work where the light source is consistent (e.g. not a mix of natural and artificial), evenly distributed (no dimmers) and directed downwards to minimise screen reflections. Walls should be a neutral colour. Obviously this is not practical for the average home user but it is something that the small business user should be aware of.

- **Warm-up time**
 The balance of colours displayed on your monitor can vary as it warms up. Allow the monitor to reach a steady temperature before adjusting it.

- **Monitor controls**
 Set the monitor controls to the optimum as recommended in the manufacturer's instructions. Once you have set the controls, tape over them to ensure that they are not accidentally moved (or changed by another user) after calibration.

- **Age**
 The phosphors used in monitors age, causing the colour spectrum to shift over time. This may mean that your monitor output no longer matches the original specification and that the original device profile is no longer appropriate. If the colour balance of your monitor is very important, you should consider replacing it at intervals.

If you're using the Serif *Colour Chart*, you can fine-tune your monitor's colour balance settings using the three reference photographs included in PagePlus's Samples\Monitor Calibration folder. MONITOR CALIBRATION.PPP includes the three images shown at right, linked as MONITORCALIB*.TIF; the Colour Chart includes a high-quality reproduction on both glossy and matte surfaced paper. Adjust your monitor's Brightness and Contrast settings as needed while referring to the greyscale samples. When you are happy with the greys, then move onto the colour settings until the display closely matches the printed photographs. Pay particular attention to the settings for the flesh tones.

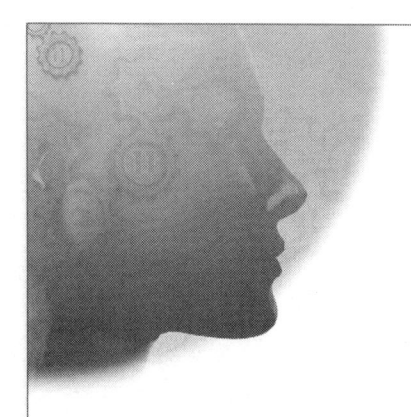

Printing your Publication

8

Printing basics

PagePlus supports scaling, tiling, colour separations, and many other useful printing options. Here we'll cover what you need to know for basic desktop printer output. If you're working with a service bureau or professional printer and need to provide PostScript output, see **Generating professional output** on p. 189 (which also covers PDF output for professional printing).

To set up your printer or begin printing:

- Click the 🖨 **Print** button on the Standard toolbar.

The Print dialog appears.

To print:

1. On the **General** tab, select a printer from the list. If necessary, click the **Properties** button to set up the printer for the correct page size, etc. Depending on your printer driver, to print text with shading or custom settings, you may need to select the **Fonts** tab and check the option to "Download TrueType Fonts as bitmap soft fonts."

2. If necessary, click the **Layout**, **Separations**, or **Prepress** tab(s) to set special print options.

    - To set options for scaling, thumbnails, multiple pages, tiling, or mail merge, select the **Layout** tab. For details, see **Printing special formats** on p. 187.

    - To specify settings for PostScript colour separations, select the **Separations** tab.

    - To set professional print options select the **Prepress** tab. See **Generating professional output** on p. 189.

3. Select the print range to be printed. If you're printing a **book**, you can select **Entire book** to output all chapters, or **Selected chapters** to output just those you selected. Whichever option you've chosen, a drop-down list lets you export all sheets in the range, or just odd or even sheets, with the option of printing in reverse order.

4. Select the number of copies.

5. The Preview window shows how your publication maps to the selected paper size. You can click the dialog's **Preview** button to hide and show the window.

Previewing the printed page

The **Print Preview** mode changes the screen view to display your layout without frames, guides, rulers, and other screen items. Special options, such as tiled output or crop marks, are not displayed.

To preview the printed page:

- Click the ![icon] **Print Preview** button on the Standard toolbar.

In Print Preview mode, the lower toolbar provides a variety of familiar view options, plus the **Multipage** button, which lets you preview your publication using a page array.

To arrange multiple pages in the preview window:

1. Click the ![icon] **Multipage** button. An array selector appears.
2. Move the pointer across the menu to choose an array, e.g. 3x2 Pages. To expand the number of choices, move the pointer to the right and downwards.

3. Click once to make your selection.

To return to single page view:

- Click the ![icon] **Multipage** button and select the "1x1 page" array.

To cancel Print Preview mode:

- Click the **Close** button.

Printing special formats

Printing booklets

PagePlus automatically performs **imposition** of folded publications when you use **File/Page Setup...** and select or define a **Folded Publications** type. The settings ensure that two or four pages of the publication are printed on each sheet of paper, with pages printed following the booklet sequence. This saves you from having to calculate how to position and collate pairs of pages on a single larger page, and lets you use automatic page numbering for the booklet pages.

To produce double-sided sheets, use your printer's double-sided option or run sheets through twice, printing first the front and then the back of the sheet (reverse top and bottom between runs). The sheets can then be collated and bound at their centre to produce a booklet, with all the pages in the correct sequence. With complex setups, you may wish to use **commercial printing**.

Printing posters and banners

Posters and banners are large-format publications where the page size extends across multiple sheets of paper. To have PagePlus take care of the printing, set up your publication beforehand using File/Page Setup... (with the **Large Publications** option) to preview and select a particular preset arrangement.

Even if the publication isn't set up as a poster or banner, you can use tiling and scaling settings (see "Tiling" below) to print onto multiple sheets from a standard size page. Each section or tile is printed on a single sheet of paper, and the various tiles can then be joined to form the complete page. To simplify arrangement of the tiles and to allow for printer margins, you can specify an overlap value.

Scaling

- Under "Special Printing" on the Print dialog's **Layout** tab, set the "As in document - % Scale factor" option to specify a custom scaling percentage. The default is 100% or normal size. To scale your work to be printed at a larger size, specify a larger value; to scale down, specify a smaller value. Check **Fit Many** to have PagePlus fit as many pages as possible on each sheet—for example, two A5 pages on a landscape A4 sheet.

- Set "Scale to fit paper size" values to adjust artwork automatically to fit neatly on the printed page.

- Note that the Fit Many option ignores printer margins, while Scale to Fit takes them into account. So if you use Fit Many, make sure your page layout borders don't extend beyond the printable region.

Printing thumbnails

- Under "Special Printing" on the Print dialog's **Layout** tab, set the "Print as thumbnails" option to print multiple pages at a reduced size on each printed sheet, taking printer margins into account. Specify the number of thumbnails per sheet in the value box.

PagePlus will print each page of the publication at a reduced size, with the specified number of small pages or "thumbnails" neatly positioned on each printed sheet.

Multiple pages

- Under "Multiple pages per Sheet" on the Print dialog's **Layout** tab, select an option.

The multiple page options are enabled when you are working with a page from the Small Publications category in Page Setup. You can select the number of times to repeat each page, and tell PagePlus to skip a certain number of regions on the first sheet of paper. Skipping regions is useful if, for example, you've already peeled off several labels from a label sheet, and don't want to print on the peeled-off sections. Check the Preview window to see how the output will look.

- If you haven't set up the publication as a Small Publication, but still want to print multiple pages per sheet, try using the **Fit Many** option (see "Scaling" above). Note that this option ignores printer margins and doesn't change the imposition (orientation) of output pages.

Tiling

- Under "Tiling" on the Print dialog's **Layout** tab, check the **Print tiled pages** option to print large (or enlarged) pages using multiple sheets of paper.

- Set the **% Scale factor** to print at a larger size (e.g. 300%)

Each section or tile is printed on a single sheet of paper; the various tiles can then be joined to form the complete page. Use this option for printing at larger sizes than the maximum paper size of your printer, typically for creating banners and posters. To simplify arrangement of the tiles and to allow for printer margins, you can specify an overlap value.

Generating professional output

Beyond printing your own copies on a desktop printer, or having copies photo-reproduced at a quick print shop, you may wish to consider professional (typically offset) printing. For example, if you need to reproduce more than about 500 copies of a piece, photocopying begins to lose its economic advantages. Or you may need **spot colour** or **process colour** printing for a particular job. You can output your PagePlus publication and hand it off to any trusted commercial printer.

If you're not using colour matching, we suggest you set up **ICC device profiles** for image colours and enable **colour management** so that images in the exported file include correct colour space information. You can also specify a device profile for your desktop printer for accurate on-screen proofing of desktop-printed colours. For details, see **Managing screen and output colours** on p. 180.

Unless you're handing off camera-ready artwork, your print provider will specify the format in which you should submit the publication: either **PDF/X** or **PostScript** (see PagePlus Help). Once you've decided whether to output as PDF or PostScript, you'll need to set Prepress options before choosing the appropriate output command.

The Separation and Pre-press options are further described in the PagePlus Help. In addition, the process for producing colour separations is detailed.

PDF/X

PDF is a format developed by Adobe to handle documents in a device- and platform-independent manner. As we pointed out in **Exporting PDF files** on p. 193, PDF excels as an electronic distribution medium and the reliable **PDF/X** formats are perfect for delivering a publication file to a professional printer. Your print partner can tell you whether to deliver PDF/X-1 or PDF/X-1a (PagePlus supports both)—but from the PagePlus end of things you won't see a difference. In either mode, all your publication's colours will be output in the CMYK colour space, and fonts you've used will be embedded. A single PDF/X file will contain all the necessary information (fonts, images, graphics, and text) your print partner requires to produce either spot or process colour separations.

To output your publication as a PDF/X file:
1. Choose **Publish as PDF...** from the File menu.
2. Review General and Advanced tab settings (see **Exporting PDF files** on p. 193).

When preparing a PDF/X file for professional printing, choose either "PDF X/1" or "PDF X/1a" in the General tab's **Compatibility** list, as advised by your print partner. Also inquire whether or not to **Impose pages**; this option is fine for desktop printing of a folded publication or one that uses facing pages, but a professional printer may prefer you to leave the imposition (page sequencing) to them.

3. Review **Prepress tab** settings.

You don't need to worry about the Compression or Security tabs; these only apply to standalone PDFs.

Saving print profiles

You can save the current combination of settings made in the Print dialog as a **print profile** with a unique name. Note that the profile includes settings from all tabs except the Separations tab. (By the way, don't confuse these PagePlus "print profiles" with ICC "device profiles.")

To save current print settings as a print profile:

- On the Print dialog's **General** tab, click the **Save As...** button next to the Print Profile list.

- Type in a new name and click **OK**.

The settings are saved as a file with the extension .PPR.

You can restore the profile later on simply by choosing its name in the list.

Using PDF

9

Exporting PDF files

PDF (short for Portable Document Format) is a cross-platform file format developed by Adobe. In a relatively short time, PDF has evolved into a worldwide standard for document distribution which works equally well for electronic or paper publishing—including professional printing. In recent years, print shops are moving away from PostScript and toward the newer, more reliable **PDF/X** formats expressly targeted for graphic arts and high quality reproduction. Several different "flavours" of PDF/X exist; PagePlus supports PDF/X-1 and PDF/X-1a.

To export your publication as a PDF file:

1. Prepare the publication following standard print publishing guidelines, and taking the distribution method into account.
2. (Optional) Insert **hyperlinks** as needed, for example to link table of contents entries to pages in the document.
3. (Optional) To create **pop-up annotations**, insert **PageHints** as needed.
4. (Optional) Once the publication is final, prepare a bookmark list (see **Creating a PDF bookmark list** on p. 195).

> NOTE: Bookmarks appear as a separate list in a special pane when the PDF file is viewed. They can link to a specific page or to an **anchor** (for example, a piece of text or a graphic object) in your publication.

5. Choose **Publish as PDF...** from the File menu and check your export settings. (To export the whole publication using default settings, you won't need to change any settings.) For a detailed explanation of each export settings see the PagePlus Help.
6. Click **OK** to proceed to export.

If you checked **Preview PDF file in Acrobat**, the resulting PDF file appears in the version of Adobe Acrobat Reader installed on your system.

Importing PDF files

It is possible to import any PDF document created with other applications directly into PagePlus to create either a new PagePlus publication or add to an existing publication. The character formatting, layout and images in the original PDF document are preserved to allow comprehensive editing of the document. To export as PDF again, simply select the **File>Publish as PDF** or use **File>Save** to save as a PagePlus publication (*.PPP).

194 | Using PDF

As well as importing a PDF document, it is also possible to append a PDF document into a currently open PDF document as new pages.

In most instances, the PDF document will import and display perfectly without any problem. However, some issues may arise which may be due to:

- font substitution issues where PagePlus may not have available the original fonts intended for the document. A warning message will indicate that fonts have been substituted automatically, although it's also possible to manage font substitution manually (see **Substituting fonts** on p. 125) after import.

- unsupported graphics or fills are present in the PDF, e.g. the .JBIG2 bitmap format or any mesh fills.

- unsupported handling, e.g. form field import.

> NOTE: PagePlus attempts to import all text, objects and graphics on a best effort basis. The diversity and complexity of PDF file contents, from a myriad of original sources, may mean that the import process cannot be guaranteed to import every page element successfully. It is suggested that the imported PDF contents are checked after every import.

To import a PDF file to create a PagePlus publication:

1. Select **File>Open**.
2. Select the name of the file, and click Open. The PDF document is imported and will repaginate to the number of pages of the original PDF document.
3. Click OK.
4. Use **File>Save** to save as a PagePlus publication (*.PPP).

To insert a PDF file into an existing PagePlus Publication:

1. Open your existing PagePlus publication.
2. Select a page (the PDF document is inserted after this page) from the Pages tab.
3. Choose **Insert>PDF File** from the Insert menu.
4. In the Open dialog, navigate to and select the PDF file for insertion. Click Open.
5. The page(s) of the PDF document are added to the PagePlus publication.

Creating a PDF bookmark list

Bookmarks are optional links that appear in a separate pane of the Adobe Reader when a PDF file is displayed. Typically, a bookmark links to a specific location such as a section heading in the publication, but it can also link to a document page. You can insert bookmarks by hand, or PagePlus can apply **automatic generation** to produce a nested bookmark list up to six levels deep, derived from named styles in your publication.

A **Bookmark Manager** enables you to view all your bookmarks at a glance, organise them into a hierarchy of entries and subentries, and modify or delete existing bookmarks as needed.

To use styles to automatically generate bookmarks:

1. Decide which named styles you want to designate as headings at each of up to six levels.
2. Check your publication to make sure these styles are used consistently.
3. Choose **Bookmark Manager...** from the Tools menu and click **Automatic....**
4. In the dialog, you'll see a list of all the style names used in your publication.
5. Check boxes to include text of a given style as a heading at a particular level (1 through 6). For example, you could include all text using the "Heading" style as a first-level heading. To remove all bookmarks in the list, clear all check boxes.
6. Click **OK** to generate bookmarks.

The mechanics of **creating a PDF bookmark list by hand** are simple. For example, to create a basic list with bookmarks to section heads, you simply proceed forward through the publication, inserting a bookmark for each heading. Bookmarking a specific location (for example, a piece of text or a graphic object) entails placing an **anchor** at that location; the anchor serves as the target for the bookmark link.

To insert bookmarks by hand:

1. (Optional) To bookmark a specific location in the publication, first place the cursor at that point or select an object. You can select a range of text (for example, a section heading) to use it as the actual text of the bookmark.
2. Choose **Bookmark Manager...** from the Tools menu. In the bookmark tree, display the entry below which you want to create the new bookmark. (Check **Create as sub-entry** if you want the new bookmark nested as a "child" of the selected entry.) Then click the **Create...** button.

3. In the Create Bookmark dialog, the **Text** field shows the range of text you selected if any (for example, a section heading). You can leave this if it's suitable for the bookmark text or edit it as needed; otherwise enter new text if the field is empty.

4. Click to select the bookmark destination type, then enter the destination.

- To bookmark a specific location, choose **An anchor in your publication**. To place a new anchor at the cursor location, select <Anchor at current selection> from the list below. You'll be prompted to enter an anchor name (with the bookmark text as the default); edit the name if you like and click **OK**. To bookmark a previously placed anchor, simply choose it from the list.

- To bookmark a specific page in the publication, select **A page in your publication** and select the target page number.

5. Click **OK** to confirm your choices.

Unlike **hyperlinks**, bookmarks also work as actual links within PagePlus publications. You can use the Bookmark Manager as a jumping-off point to any bookmarked entry.

Using PDF Forms

The continuing development of Adobe's® Acrobat® technology means that great new possibilities are available to PagePlus. One of the most exciting is the use of electronic-based PDF forms—these allow information to be collected from readers of your publication in an efficient and modern manner. In much the same way as traditional paper forms are used to collect information (remember your last Tax Return!), PDF forms offer the same form completion concepts, but increase the interactivity between publisher and audience by using an electronic medium.

Some common form types are:

- Application forms
- Contact Information forms
- Request forms
- Feedback forms
- Guest books

One thing in common with all PDF forms is that they have to be published as PDF to operate. A PagePlus .PPP file with form functionality must be converted to PDF with **File>Publish as PDF**.

Form Structure

The building blocks of a form comprise a mixture of text, graphics and **Form fields**. Form fields collect recipient data and can be added, moved and modified in a similar way to more familiar objects in PagePlus such as graphics and table elements. A field can be a Text field, Radio Button, Combo box, List box, Check box or a simple button.

```
FirstName: [                    ]

LastName: [                    ]

   Gender:
      ⦿ Male   ⦿ Female
Pick Event:  [Social Events    ▼]

Send more information ? [✓]

        [ Submit ]  [ Reset ]
```

From the form recipient's perspective, information is typed into text boxes or selected from check boxes, radio buttons, or drop-down boxes. The information entered can be numeric, textual, or a mixture of both.

Each field has its own set of **Form Field Properties** relating to its appearance, its value(s), validation, calculations, and the action expected of the field.

In PagePlus, the form should be integrated into your Page design as you develop your publication (see **Designing your PDF Forms** on p.198). The form's functionality only then becomes active when a PDF of the form is generated. When a form recipient enters data into form fields the data can be collected as described below.

Javascript is used to allow interactivity in your PDF forms. It drives formatting, **validation**, calculations, and actions—all key functions in PDF form development.

How is data collected?

Several methods exist for collecting forms once they have been completed.

(1) By Hardcopy **Print**.

(2) You can **Save Data to e-mail** (alternatively you can save data within the form).

(3) You can **Submit Data to Web** (a CGI application; by submission to a web-enabled server/database).

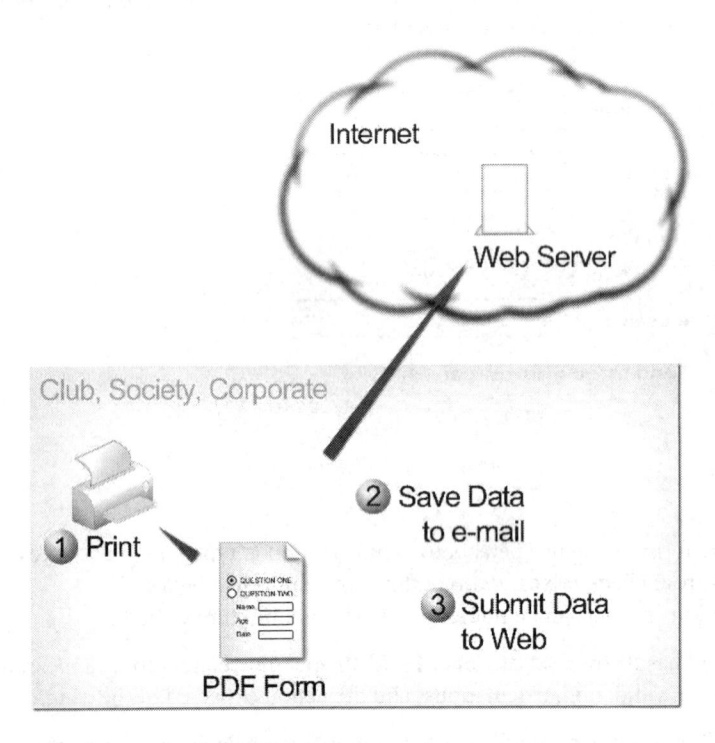

Designing your PDF forms

Things to do for successful form design:

- Decide on the information (form data) you want to collect.
- Map out your design on some paper, keeping usability and visual appeal in mind.
- Choose a form size and structure (single or multi-page).

- Create the form's background including graphics, text and other static objects.
- Add your form fields with correct alignment and sizing.
- Test, test and test again by using **Publish as PDF**.

> TIP: To preserve your form design, remember to check the Embed fonts option in the Advanced tab.

Using ruler guides

One of the most important design tips is to lay out your ruler guides correctly. A combination of good guide layout and alignment or distribution of form fields makes the design process a lot simpler. See **Using the rulers** on p. 41 for more information.

Arranging form fields

Form fields can be arranged in the same way that other objects in PagePlus can be arranged. **Ordering**, **aligning**, **distributing** and **resizing** are all possible.

Sizing

You may have already tried adding a form object of standard size by simply clicking on the Form toolbar entry and then on the page—a quick and easy way to build up your form structure.

> TIP: It's also possible to select your form object but to then drag your mouse cursor across the page to draw out the form field to your preferred size and shape.

Some Form fields may not need to be the standard size—a numeric field to support a maximum of three digits doesn't need to be 25 characters wide! Fortunately, all form fields in PagePlus have resize handles which you can drag in any direction. See **Resizing objects** on p. 57.

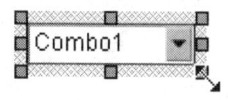

Placing Submit and Reset buttons

For Web-ready forms, the general practice is to place your Submit and Reset buttons together at the end of your form. This will help to prevent premature completion of your form.

Locking form fields

Happy with your form field positioning? To prevent you from accidentally moving your beautifully positioned form fields, you can lock single or multiple form fields by right-clicking on the field(s) and selecting **Arrange>Lock Objects** from the drop-down menu.

Arranging tab order

The recipients of PDF forms have two options for navigating their forms—by clicking in each field in turn (using the mouse) or using the Tab key to jump from field to field. The latter method is more efficient as forms are generally designed to be completed in a sequential manner.

This tab sequence is governed by the chronological order in which the form designer adds the form fields to the page during the design process. Clearly, the form design may change during development so the tab order is prone to getting out of sequence.

Fortunately, the **Tab Order** button on the **Form** toolbar can be used to reset the tab order at the end of the design process.

To change tab order:

1. Click the **Tab Order** button. This reveals blue tab markers on all your form fields.

2. Sequentially, click on the form fields in the order in which you want them to be assigned tab numbers. This automatically assigns a new tab number to the blue marker—your first click will be to assign 1 in First Name field, the second click 2 in the Last Name field, etc.

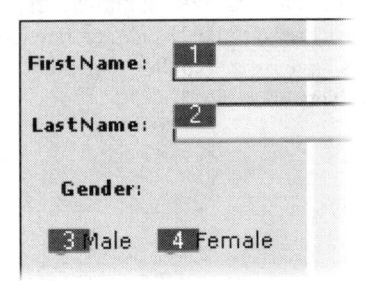

   ```
   First Name:  [1]
   Last Name:   [2]
      Gender:
              [3] Male   [4] Female
   ```

3. Click the **Tab Order** button again to switch off the blue tab markers.

If you're not happy with the order you've assigned, click the **Tab Order** button and start again.

Creating PDF forms

Previously, in **Designing your PDF Forms**, we looked at PDF Form layout. Let's now look at actually creating a PDF form. We'll focus on the addition of form fields to the page and subsequent field labelling—the addition of supporting text and graphics to the form is covered previously.

Adding form fields

A series of form fields can be added to the page, depending on the type of form you want to create. Typically a mix of form fields will make up your finished form design.

Fields are created from the **Form** toolbar or via **Insert>Form Field**. You assign an internal unique name to each field and then set a variety of properties. Each form field has its own set of **Form Field Properties** which can be modified to suit your form implementation.

Icon	Form Field Name	When to use?
	Button*	Use when specifying an action that can be triggered by a button click.
	Submit button*	Use when sending the form recipient's completed form data to Serif Web Resources or to your own Web server. A Form Submit Wizard is activated to enable quick and easy button setup.
	Reset button*	Use when you want to add a button to clear all form fields of data (often complements the above Submit button).
	Print button*	Use when you want to add a print button to your form.
	Check Box	Ideal when you want to multiply select a series of options displayed side by side. A good alternative to a Combo Box or List box if space allows.
	Text Field	Use for adding text, numbers or a mixture of both.

202 | Using PDF

Combo Box	For selection from a scrollable list of items in a drop-down menu where only one item can be selected. The box also allows data entry to be input into this box type. Smaller than a List Box.
List Box	For selection from a scrollable list of items; supports multiple selection and advanced actions on selection of menu items.
Radio Button	Good for selection of a single mutually exclusive item from a grouped subset of choices.
Signature	Used for the digital signing of secure documents.

* This button shares a drop down menu with other buttons marked with an asterisk. The button type previously chosen will always be display on the Form toolbar.

To add a form field:

1. Select one of the form field buttons on the **Form** toolbar.
2. Move your cursor to the location at which you want to place your form field and click once.
3. Right-click on the form field and choose **Form Field Properties** from the drop-down menu.
4. In the **General** tab, overwrite the current **Name** with a unique internal name. You can also choose several other optional settings (see General tab).
5. Go to the **Options** tab, and choose enter a new Caption name.
6. (Optional) Go to the **Actions** tab and click the **Add** button.
7. (Optional) In the resulting Action dialog, select an Event that will be used to trigger the action.
8. (Optional) Choose an **Action** from the drop-down menu.
9. (Optional) Change the properties displayed under the selected action. The options shown change depending to the action selected.

Buttons

A whole range of buttons of varying design and function can be created. Some examples include:

- Advanced - Displays menu options that are only applicable for advanced uses.
- Show All - Displays all menu options.
- Next page - Jumps the form recipient to the next page.
- Open - Opens a file or Web link.
- Import - Imports form data.
- Reset - Clears all form data. Preset available.
- Print - sends the form to a configured printer. Preset available.

The button is specifically designed to run a Form Submit Wizard. This ensures that configuration of Web-ready forms is made that much easier.

Check box

Check boxes are boxes containing a simple check, cross, or other symbol. The form recipient clicks once to select or deselect the box.

Example:

Would you like to be notified of any upcoming events in the near future?

Text field

Text fields are used for entering input, either textual or numerical. **Validation** can be performed on any text field.

Example:

Name, Address, Cash amounts, Phone Numbers.

For large text fields remember to check the **Multiline** check box to allow line breaking.

Combo box

The Combo Box presents a list of menu items in a drop-down menu, and optionally allows the form recipient to enter their own items.

Example:

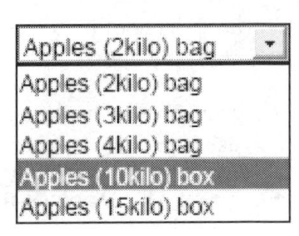

Apples (2kilo) bag   Click on drop   Apples (2kilo) bag
                     down to   Apples (2kilo) bag
                     expand   Apples (3kilo) bag
                     Combo Box   Apples (4kilo) bag
                                      Apples (10kilo) box
                                      Apples (15kilo) box

List box

The List Box presents a list of items in a static box with scrollbar support. Multiple selection of items is supported.

You can also use Commit on Select to run Javascript scripts when you select menu items. This is ideal when you want to display supporting pictures or sounds with your menu items.

For example, to select Andy Brown, Jason Orange and Paul Black, use Ctrl-click on the menu items:

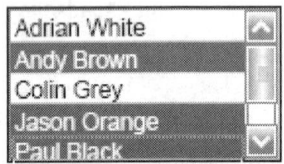

Adrian White
Andy Brown
Colin Grey
Jason Orange
Paul Black

Radio buttons

Radio buttons operate slightly differently to other form fields. To operate correctly, Radio buttons which are intended to be grouped, e.g. for Male/Female Gender selection, must both be configured to be a part of the same configurable Field Group. Field groups are set in Form Field Properties, General tab.

For example, in a field group called "group1" you could include radio buttons as Yes/No options:

○ Yes   ● No

Alternatively, you could have another set of radio buttons, in a different field group (called "Gender"), which can determine the sex of the form recipient.

● Male   ○ Female

Radio buttons can be ○ unchecked (default) or ● checked. For checked buttons, use the **Checked by default** option on Form Field Properties (Options tab).

Using field labelling

For the form field types Check box, Text field, Combo box, List box, or Radio button, it doesn't make much sense to add the form field to the page without some form of labelling. This indicates to the form recipient what the associated field relates to, e.g. a Radio button or Check box without an accompanying description is clearly pointless.

> NOTE: The Button form field has built-in labelling it adopts the Caption field as its label.

> TIP: For good form design, ensure that labelling is positioned consistently and is placed close enough to the form field to avoid confusion.

To apply labels:

- Add your label as Artistic Text (see **Using artistic text** on p. 78). This lets you apply standalone text, allowing greater flexibility.
- Group the label and form field together.
- Right-click and select **Arrange>Align Objects** from the drop-down menu. Choose a vertical or horizontal alignment option, and select a distribute objects option.

Form field properties

Form field properties control how the form field will operate when the form recipient enters their input. A series of tabs are arranged so that some tabs, e.g. **General**, **Appearance**, **Options**, or **Actions**, are common to all the form fields but others, such as **Format**, **Validation** and **Calculations** are only displayed for text fields and combo boxes.

To access Form Field Properties:
1. Double-click the form field.
2. Click on one of several tabs: General, Appearance, Options, Actions, Validate, or Calculate.
3. Click the **OK** or **Cancel** button to exit the dialog.

See PagePlus help for a description of each of the tabs.

Publishing your PDF Form

Once your PDF form is completed you can publish the form using **File>Publish as PDF**. See **Exporting PDF files** on p. 193.

> NOTE: If you Publish as PDF using PDF/X-1 or PDF/X-1a compatibility, any PDF form fields present will be converted to graphics and will not be available. Choose an Acrobat option instead.

Validating data entry

Once you have designed your form, added form fields, and supporting text you can configure some data entry rules, i.e. validation, on your form fields. The main objective is to ensure that the form is filled out correctly. This is done by checking that data entered into each field is of the correct format, structure and sequence.

> NOTE: the form cannot be submitted until validation is successful.

Validation of Formats

The **Format** tab for text fields and combo boxes performs validation in that the format of each form field can be restricted to a set structure and sequence.

Text fields can be made to display:

- a **Number** with differing decimal place settings, separators, or currency symbols. Negative numbers can made distinct from positive numbers.
- a **Date** of varying date formats, with differing delimiter types.
- a **Time** of varying time formats.
- a **Custom** format as dictated by a custom Format and Keystroke javascript.

Simple Validation

For numeric fields you can apply Simple Validation to restrict the number range input by setting a **Minimum** and **Maximum value**.

Custom Validation with Javascript

More advanced validation on PDF forms can be performed within PagePlus. It's possible to develop your own Javascript code and apply it within the Validation tab of text fields and combo boxes. When the form field is completed by the form recipient, the custom script is run and validation is carried out.

Some examples of custom validation include:

- the blocking of swear words.
- Specifying account numbers with a set structure (e.g., EM 158 3466 7546//2).

The development of Javascript code is outside the scope of this document. However, a useful starting point is the **Acrobat JavaScript Scripting Reference Guide** available from www.adobe.com.

> NOTE: Some custom Javascript may not be supported by versions of Acrobat Reader. Serif recommends that you test all forms in Acrobat software used by your target audience.

Collecting data from forms

Via Hardcopy Printout

This is a simple fill-in and print to hardcopy solution. This is great if your form recipients are located together, perhaps in the same office.

WARNING: If using Acrobat® Reader®, any completed form data will be lost when you close your completed PDF form. Exceptions exist when using Standard or Professional software.

Within the PDF File

Alternatively, it is possible to store form data within the PDF Form itself by using the **Save** or **Save As...** command. One condition of this is that the form recipient must be using one of the following versions of Acrobat software:

- Adobe® Acrobat® 6.0 (or later) Standard or Professional
- Adobe® Acrobat® 7.0 Elements

> NOTE: Acrobat® Reader® software (6.0 and above) is unable to save form data within the form. However, for form recipients with Acrobat® Reader® 7.0 software, **Adobe® LiveCycle™ Reader Extensions** software is available from Adobe which will permit form data to be saved locally with the form. This is called rights-based PDF Form handling.

If you can save data within the PDF form then it's clear that you can E-mail the completed form to the form originator. With the completed form still open, use **File>E-mail** to send the E-mail to the intended recipient.

Via the Web

Your PDF Form can be configured to be Web ready by passing completed form data to a CGI application on a Web server. This would typically be a server-sided web page designed to process the data and pass it to either a text file, database or other storage location. As an example, new subscriber details, collected via a PDF Form, can be sent automatically to a previously configured "subscribers" database.

All Web-ready forms have one thing in common—they must be submitted to allow data to be collected. Typically, you may have come across this on web sites when you enter details into a form then submit the data by pressing a Submit button. The same applies for PDF forms—a **Submit** button can be configured in order to submit the form data to the Web server. You can either create the button unaided or use the **Form Submit Wizard** (see below). Either way, the use of the submit process is the major difference between web-ready and other less dynamic forms.

The Web process, as mentioned, requires a Web server to operate. Not everyone will have access to or even want to operate their own Web server so, as an alternative to this, you can use **Serif Web Resources**. This is a free Web to e-mail gateway service which will collect your valued form data at Serif and send it to your E-mail address—the service does require that you firstly have a Customer login (for security reasons), which will allow you to create, edit and delete Form IDs via a web page accessible from the Wizard. The Form ID, a unique 30-digit number, is required for Serif Web Resources to operate and is generated automatically when you enter your destination e-mail address in the above web page.

> NOTE: No personal data will be stored on Serif Web servers. All form data is redirected in real time.

Submitting Form Data

The submission of form data sounds a very complicated operation but by using a **Form Submit Wizard** the process is relatively straightforward. The Wizard not only creates a Submit button for your form, but configures the underlying submit process and the format in which your form data is to be stored in.

The submit process is made either to Serif Web Resources or to your own Web server address (e.g., http://testserver.global.com/forms/collect.asp).

Using PDF | 209

Form data can be stored in several data formats:

Data Format	via Serif Web Resources	To Web Server
HTML	ASCII. The form data can be read directly in your e-mail without acrobat software.	ASCII. Use for sending form data directly to the Server-sided Databases, as in Web forms.
FDF	The form data is e-mailed as an attachment, and when opened, is reunited with the original form to allow data to be read In Situ.	binary. The form data can be stored on the web server.
XFDF	As for FDF but with additional XML-based support.	binary. The form data can be stored on the web server.
PDF	The form data and the original form are e-mailed together as a single PDF and appear as an attachment.	binary. The form data can be stored on the web server. Useful for preserving **digital signatures**.

To run the Form Submit Wizard:

1. Select the ![icon] **Form Submit Wizard** from the Button flyout menu on the **Form** toolbar.
2. In the first step, start the wizard by clicking the Next> button.
3. Choose either Serif Web Resources or your own server as the destination of your form recipient's data. The Serif Web Resources option is appropriate if you don't have access to your own web server. Depending on your choice, you can:

   1. **For Serif Web Resources**, click Next>.
   2. Click the **Get a Form ID** button to display Serif's customer login web page. This page is where you log onto your customer account to enter firstly your e-mail address to send form data to, and secondly to generate a unique Form ID for use in the secure e-mail communication.
   3. At the web page, if you already have a customer login you can enter your e-mail address and password. For new customer you must register before continuing.
   4. After login, select the **add form** link to enter the e-mail address that you want your form data to be sent to.
   5. Click the **Add Form** button. This generates an entry in the displayed list from which a 30-digit Form ID can be copied.
   6. Paste the Form ID directly from the web page into the input field in your Wizard dialog.
   7. Click the Next> button.
   8. Select a Data format from the drop-down menu that you would like to store and transport your form data. Select one of: HTML, FDF, PDF or XFDF (see above).

OR

1. **For your own Web server**, click Next>.
2. Add your Web Server address to the displayed field, click Next>.

> NOTE: this should not be a file directory but a valid Web site on the Intranet/Internet.

3. Choose a data format for exporting the form data. Select one of: HTML, FDF, PDF or XFDF (see above). NOTE: You must ensure that your server is able to process the above data formats.
4. Finish the Wizard process by clicking the **Finish** button.
4. Move your cursor to the location for your button and click once.

> TIP: Use the Reset button available as a preset on the Form toolbar.

> NOTE: The Submit button settings can be edited as for other form fields by right-clicking and selection of Form Field Properties. This will allow form fields to be included/excluded from data collection.

Importing form data (FDF only)

It's possible to import form data which has previously been submitted into another PDF Form. The original form data must have been submitted in FDF format. A great way of doing this is to create a button, which when pressed will automatically populate the form fields on your PDF Form. This means the form originator can exactly replicate how the form was originally filled in—a very important feature when dealing with contractual, legal or financial forms.

To create an import button:

1. Select the button option from the **Form** toolbar.
2. Move your cursor to the location for your button and click once.
3. Right-click on the button and choose **Form Field Properties** from the drop-down menu.
4. Overwrite the current Name with, e.g. "import". This assigns an internal name to the form field.

5. Go to the Options tab, and choose enter a new Caption name. Enter a suitable import text, e.g. "Import Form Data".
6. Go to the **Actions** tab and click the **Add** button. This adds the action to the list.
7. In the resulting Action dialog, ensure that **On MouseUp** is selected as an Event.
8. Choose **Import form data** as an **Action** from the drop-down menu.
9. Click the **Browse...** button and navigate to the FDF file that is to be imported.
10. Click the **OK** button.

Understanding export values

Export values are used in Web-ready forms where menu items in Combo or List Box can be assigned a unique value. The export value is passed to and interpreted by the Web server when the form is submitted. If no export value is set then the menu item name is used.

> NOTE: You only need to set the Export value if you are sending the data to a web-enabled database across your Intranet or the Internet.

Export values can be modified in Form Field Properties, Options tab for the above control types.

For example, a Combo box may have replacement export values assigned as well as the menu items:

Menu item	Export Value
Apples (2kilo) bag	1
Apples (3kilo) bag	2
Apples (4kilo) bag	3
Apples (10kilo) box	4
Apples (15kilo) box	5
Apples (20kilo) box	6

Using Digital signatures

The increase in the need for security in electronic documentation has bought about the development of **Digital Signatures**. A fundamental requirement to preserve the authenticity and integrity of an author's documents is met with this technology.

- For the form designer, it's possible to certify documents as well as sign them. This process ensures that the form is certified by the author, but also dictates the changes that can be made when the form is completed by recipients.

- For the form recipient, in the same way that a hardcopy form can be signed, e.g. to authorise or to agree to terms and conditions, the recipient can verify and then digitally sign documents previously certified or signed by an author.

From the form designer's perspective, signing functionality has to be built into PDF Forms by creating a **Signature** form field (see below), irrespective of whether you are certifying the PDF form or not.

To create a Digital Signature field in your PDF Form:

1. Select the [icon] **Signature** option from the **Form** toolbar.

2. Move your cursor to the location for your button and click once. The signature field is displayed, i.e.

3. Right-click on the field and choose **Form Field Properties** from the drop-down menu.

4. Overwrite the current **Name** with a new internal name for the form field.

When the form is published using **Publish as PDF**, the signature field is activated but remains unsigned, i.e.

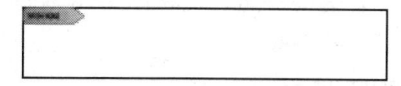

Double clicking on this field permits certifying and **digital signing** as described below.

Certifying your PDF document

As a document's author, you can attest to the contents of the PDF form when published, and also specify the types of changes permitted (if any) on the document.

A Digital ID containing a signature must be set up to allow your PDF Form to be certified; this ID is shared with your PDF form recipients in a certificate. The ID is purchased either from a third-party signature handler (e.g. Entrust, Geotrust, RSA security, Verisign) or you can choose to have a self-signed digital ID.

> NOTE: To certify a PDF form you must be operating Adobe Acrobat 5.01 or later (i.e., not Acrobat Reader software).

The Signature field and Signature tab appears with a blue ribbon icon when the PDF Form is certified.

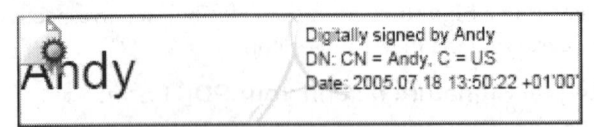

Andy
Digitally signed by Andy
DN: CN = Andy, C = US
Date: 2005.07.18 13:50:22 +01'00'

To certify a PDF Form:

1. Save your form as a PDF with **File>Publish as PDF**.
2. Double-click your created **Signature** field in the displayed PDF Form.
3. In the **Alert - document is not Certified** dialog, select the **Certify Document** button.
4. Choose an allowable action for the PDF such as **Only allowing form fill-ins and commenting**.
5. If you don't have a Digital ID:
   1. Click the Add Digital ID button in the Data Exchange File - Digital ID Selection dialog.
   2. Create the digital ID from your chosen source (Default or Windows Certificate Security, or third party).
   3. Select Save as Certified Document.

OR:

If you already have a Digital ID:

1. In the Sign dialog, select a reason for signing the document in the drop-down menu.

2. Select Sign and Save as or Sign and Save.

Digitally signing forms

Typically, a PDF Form previously certified and circulated by the author, can be signed by one or more recipient to indicate acknowledgement, acceptance of the forms' contents, etc.

If the form is certified the recipient will be informed if the form is still valid or not.

> **NOTE:** To digitally sign a PDF form you must be operating Adobe Acrobat 5.01 or later (i.e., not Acrobat Reader software).

To digitally sign a PDF Form:

1. Double-click your created **Signature** field in the displayed PDF Form.

2. In the "Alert - document is not Certified" dialog, select the **Continue Signing** button.

3. Choose a reason for signing such as **I have reviewed this document**.

4. Select Sign and Save as or Sign and Save.

There are two signature types that can be signed: Text (shown below) or Graphic.

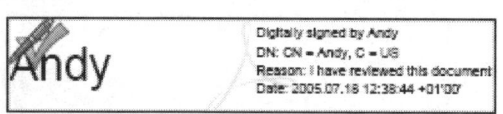

```
Andy          Digitally signed by Andy
              DN: CN = Andy, C = US
              Reason: I have reviewed this document
              Date: 2005.07.18 12:38:44 +01'00'
```

You can view full signature information on the Signature tab.

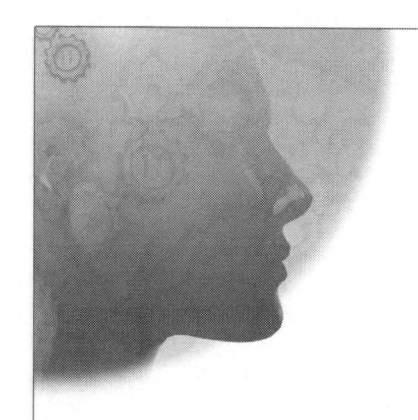

Producing Web Pages

10

Getting started in Web mode

How easy is it to create your own Web site with PagePlus? It can be as simple as selecting a preset design template and editing the headings and accompanying text. And no matter how much customising you choose to do after that, the whole job won't be nearly as complicated as developing your own site from first principles. So, if you're already comfortable using PagePlus for paper publications, you'll find it easy going. If you're just beginning, you'll learn to use PagePlus tools as you go.

Essentially, PagePlus takes the pages you've laid out and converts them to HTML. In fact, the Web design templates simplify things further by providing you with a variety of starter layouts, professionally designed expressly for World Wide Web display.

Starting a new Web publication

Paper Publishing mode is the familiar PagePlus environment for creating print publications. However, before developing your web site PagePlus must operate in **Web Publishing mode**. The Web Publishing mode includes special features, such as menu items and custom settings, to facilitate creation of World Wide Web pages.

> **TIP:** If you choose any of the Web Page Design Templates after starting PagePlus you will be in Web Publishing mode automatically.

To create a new Web publication using a Page Wizard:

1. Launch PagePlus or choose **New...** from the File menu. You'll see the Startup Wizard.

2. Select the **Use a design template** option, select a Web-based publication category (e.g., Websites) on the left, and examine the samples on the right. Click the sample that's closest to what you want, then click **Finish**.

Just as in Paper Publishing mode, you also have the option of starting a new publication from scratch, or opening an existing publication.

If you'd like to build on previous work you've done with PagePlus, you can also take an existing paper publication and convert it to a Web publication.

To turn an existing PagePlus (paper) publication into a World Wide Web site:

- Open the publication in Paper Publishing mode and choose **Switch to Web Publishing** from the File menu.

Hyperlinking an object

Hyperlinking an object such as a box or **QuickButton**, a word, or a picture means that a visitor to your Web site can click on the object to trigger an event. The event might be a jump to a Web page (either on your site or somewhere else on the Web), the appearance of an e-mail composition window, or the display of a graphic, text, audio, or video file. Hyperlinking enables visitors to navigate through your Web site or **PDF document**.

To hyperlink an object:

1. Use the Pointer tool to highlight the region of text.

2. Click the **Hyperlink** button on the Standard toolbar. The Hyperlinks dialog appears.

3. Click to select the link destination type, and enter the specific hyperlink target—an Internet page, A page on your Web site, an email address or local file.

4. Click **OK**.

As a visual cue, hyperlinked words are underlined and appear in the colour you've specified in the Scheme Manager (see **Choosing Web site colours** on p. 224).

To modify or remove a hyperlink:

1. Use the Pointer tool to select the object, or click for an insertion point inside the linked text. (It's not necessary to drag over a hyperlinked region of text.)

2. Click the **Hyperlink** button on the Standard toolbar. The Hyperlinks dialog appears with the current link target shown. If the link is in text, the whole text link highlights.

- To modify the hyperlink, select a new link destination type and/or target.

- To remove the hyperlink, click the **Remove** button.

> NOTE: Removing a hyperlink does not remove the underlying object or text.

Viewing hyperlinks in your publication

The **Hyperlink Manager** gives you an overview of all the hyperlinks in your publication.

To display the Hyperlink Manager:

- Choose **Hyperlink Manager...** from the Tools menu.

The Hyperlink Manager dialog displays both object and text hyperlinks in your publication, listed by page number. The entries are in "from/to" format, showing each link's source object type and its destination page or URL.

To display a hyperlink for closer inspection:

- Click to select the link entry and click the **Display** button. Double-click the link entry.

To remove or modify a hyperlink:

- Click to select the link entry and click the **Remove** or **Modify** button. To modify the hyperlink, select a new link destination type and/or target.

Adding hotspots

A hotspot is a transparent hyperlink region on a Web page. Usually placed on top of images, hotspots act like "buttons" that respond when clicked in a Web browser. They are especially useful if you want the visitor to be able to click on different parts of a picture (such as a graphic "menu" or map of your site).

To define a hotspot:

1. Choose **Web Object** from the Insert menu and select **Hotspot** from the submenu.
2. Click and drag to draw a rectangular hotspot region. The Hyperlinks dialog appears.
3. Click to select the link destination type, and enter the specific hyperlink target—an Internet page, A page on your Web site, an email address or local file.
4. Click **OK**.

To modify a hotspot hyperlink:

- Using the Pointer tool, double-click the hotspot.
  OR

  Click to select the hotspot, then click the ![icon] **Hyperlink** button on the Standard toolbar.

The Hyperlinks dialog appears with the current hotspot link target shown.

- To modify the hyperlink, select a new link destination type and/or target.
- To remove the hyperlink, click the **Remove** button.

Editing hotspots

You can move and resize hotspots on the page, just like other objects. A selected hotspot has both an outer bounding box and an inner outline, which serve different purposes.

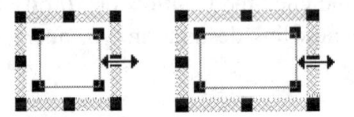

To move or resize a hotspot:

- Click to select the hotspot.
- To move, drag from the centre, or from the hotspot's bounding box. To constrain the hotspot to vertical or horizontal movement, hold down the **Shift** key while dragging.
- To resize, drag on its outer (bounding box) handles.

By editing the inner outline, you can convert rectangular hotspots into freeform shapes that closely match the parts of the underlying graphic you want to be "hot." To edit the outline, first move the mouse pointer over the hotspot's inner outline until the cursor changes to indicate whether you're over a node or a line.

Adding rollovers

The term **rollover** refers to an interaction between a mouse and a screen object. For example, you can point your mouse at a graphic (such as a navigation bar button) on a Web page, and see it instantly change colour or become a different picture. When you point to a Web page object, your mouse pointer physically enters the screen region occupied by the object.

This triggers an event called a "mouseover" which can trigger some other event—such as swapping another image into the same location. An object whose appearance changes through image-swapping in response to mouse events is called a **rollover graphic**.

You can directly import rollover graphics created in Serif DrawPlus (see PagePlus Help for more information).

Rollover options

Adding rollovers is basically a matter of deciding which rollover state(s) you'll want to define for a particular object, then specifying an image for each state. PagePlus provides four basic choices:

- **Normal** is the "resting" state of the graphic before any rollover, and is always defined.

- **Over** is the state triggered by a mouseover— when the mouse pointer is directly over the object.

- **Down** is triggered by a mouse click on the graphic.

- **Down+Over** implies a mouseover that occurs when the graphic is already Down, i.e. after it's been clicked.

You'll also have the option of specifying a **hyperlink** event—for example, a jump to a targeted Web page—that will trigger if the user clicks on the object. And you can even group buttons on a page so they work together and only one at a time can be down.

To create a rollover graphic:

1. In a suitable image-editing program, create the variant source images for each state you'll be defining. (See **Creating variant source images** on p. 224.)

2. Choose **Web Object** from the Insert menu and select **Rollover...** from the submenu.

3. Specify which rollover states (see above) you want to activate for each graphic by checking boxes in the Rollover Graphic dialog. For each one, use the **Browse** button to locate the corresponding source image.

4. Check **Embed files in site** if you want to incorporate the image(s) in the PagePlus file.

5. Check either **Normal** or **Down** as the button's initial rollover state.

6. Click **Set...** to define a hyperlink target for the button. (For details, see **Hyperlinking an object** on p. 220.)
7. Check **Radio button** if you want to link all the buttons (on a given page) that have this option checked, so that only one of them at a time can be down.
8. Click **OK**. The first time you define a rollover state, you'll see rollover layers established in the document (see below).

To edit a rollover graphic:
1. Right-click the graphic and choose **Edit Rollover....**
2. Make new selections as needed and click **OK**.

Creating variant source images

For each object with at least one activated rollover state, you'll need to provide a source image. It's the often subtle differences between the Normal image and the "variants" that make the object appear to switch from one state to another. For example, if you've checked the "Over" state for an object, you need to include a variant image that the Web page can display when the button is moused over. If you want the button's text to change from black to yellow, then the "Over" state will need an image with yellow text.

Choosing Web site colours

Like all PagePlus publications, each Web publication has a colour scheme, selected by using the **Schemes** tab. Each scheme has a name and consists of five complementary basic colours which you can apply to any design element. (For details, see **Using colour schemes** on p. 169.) A selection of schemes (named "WWW 1" through "WWW 9") are specifically designed for Web use.

Web colours

Web publications also have several special **Web colour** settings, usually defined as part of a colour scheme in the **Scheme Manager**. You'll need to know about these, even if you haven't applied scheme colours to other elements in your publication:

- The **Hyperlink** colour applies to hyperlinked text before it's been clicked on, while the same text after a visitor has clicked to "follow" the link takes on the **Followed Hyperlink** colour.

- A Web site's **Background** is a solid colour with the option of overlaying a tiled (repeated) picture, usually a bitmap pattern. The tiled picture option works just like desktop "wallpaper," so a small bitmap can go a long way. The colour scheme sample shows ![icon] if the scheme uses a tiled bitmap. If you use a picture background with transparent regions, the Background colour is still active and will show through; otherwise the picture will cover the background colour.

In Web Publishing mode, colour scheme samples in the Schemes tab show the Web colours along with the five basic scheme colours, as shown at left.

The easiest way to apply new Web colours is to select a different colour scheme by clicking a sample on the **Schemes** tab. You can also change any of the Web colours within a scheme using the Scheme Manager, in the same way that you would modify the scheme's five basic colours. See **Using Colour Schemes** on p. 169.

Setting custom page backgrounds

The Web colours defined in the Scheme Manager normally apply throughout the site, but you can override the Scheme Manager's Background picture/picture setting for any particular page.

To set a custom page background:

1. Choose **Web Site Properties...** from the File menu.
2. On the dialog's Background tab, uncheck **Use Scheme Manager settings** and set new options for **Page colour** and/or **Use picture**.

> NOTE: The settings apply only to the current page.

Setting Web picture display options

When you export a publication as a Web site, PagePlus applies certain global settings to determine how each image—whether drawn, pasted in, or imported—ends up as a separate bitmap displayed on the Web page.

The following conversion settings are used for Web publishing:

- Each image in the publication is exported as a separate file.

- Any image you inserted as a GIF or JPEG is exported as the original file, using its original file name.

- Inserted PNG images, metafiles, and all other graphics are converted to JPEG images, using a compression quality setting of 10 (low compression, high detail). For these images, PagePlus automatically generates file names, using incremental numbering (IMG1, IMG2, etc.) that continues each time you export.

Global export options and setting export formats are described in more detail in the PagePlus Help.

Choosing page properties

There's more to creating a successful Web site than designing the pages. It's a good idea to browse the **Site Properties** dialog, accessible from **File>Web Site Properties** and review a variety of settings you might not otherwise have considered! This section covers settings on the Page tab.

Site Properties/Page tab

Some of the options on the dialog's **Page** tab pertain just to the current page, while others apply to the site as a whole. The Web page **title**, which will appear in the title bar of the visitor's Web browser, can serve to unify the pages and focus the site's identity, as well as aid navigation. Each page in your site can have its own title, but you may prefer to use the same title on multiple pages (in effect, a site title). An easy way to do this is to start with a blank page, give it a title, then replicate that page. Copies of that page will have the same title.

Each page also has a **file name** when it's published. You can specify file names individually; otherwise PagePlus will automatically generate them. Check the instructions from your Web service provider as to their naming conventions for Home Pages and file extensions. By default, PagePlus names your first (Home) page INDEX.HTML—the standard file name a browser will be looking for. Depending on the particular server in use, however, some other name may be required. Likewise, the extension .HTM is sometimes used for pages.

Adding animation effects

PagePlus lets you add two varieties of eye-catching animation effects to any Web page: **animated marquees** and **GIF animations**. Either way, you can preview the animation and/or customise the effect. Once placed into your Web publication, the animations appear static, but they will spring to life once the site has been exported and a visitor views your page in a Web browser.

The **Animated Marquee Wizard** prompts you through the steps of adding horizontally scrolling motion to a headline or catch phrase. You can choose the background colour, enter from one to three lines of text, and define text properties, scroll direction, speed and alignment for each line. If you like, you can define a URL hyperlink for the marquee. For the most compelling effect, select two lines with strongly contrasting text colours and opposing scroll directions.

Inserting an animated GIF is just like inserting a static picture (see **Importing images** on p. 131 for more details). PagePlus lets you preview, then pick and choose animations. Use them to illustrate particular themes or just add some fun to your page!

Adding sound and video

PagePlus lets you augment your Web pages with sound and video files in a variety of standard formats, including both **non-streaming** and **streaming** media. (Non-streaming files must download in entirety to a user's computer before they begin playing; streaming files require a special player that buffers incoming data and can start playing before the whole clip has arrived.)

Please see the PagePlus Help for more information.

Adding Java applets

Java is a cross-platform, object-oriented programming language used to create mini-applications called **applets** that can be attached to Web pages and that run when the page is viewed in a Web browser. PagePlus lets you add Java applets to your Web publications. You don't have to write your own! Plenty of applets are available online—for example animation, interface components, live information updating, two-way interaction, and many more.

Downloaded applets typically consist of a main ".class" file and one or more associated files (such as other .class files, picture files, media files, etc.). Again, you don't need to understand the underlying code, but it's essential to make sense of any "Read Me" documentation that comes with the applet. When using PagePlus to embed an applet, you must list its component files as well as any necessary parameters (as described in the applet's documentation) that specify exactly how the applet should run.

When adding a Java applet in PagePlus, you have the option of **embedding** its files in your publication, as opposed to keeping them separate. Although embedding any file adds to the size of the publication, it is the default option because you'll no longer have to worry about juggling separate files or the chance of accidentally deleting one of them.

When you publish your site, PagePlus takes care of exporting and copying both embedded and non-embedded files.

PagePlus inserts a marker into your publication at the place where the applet will appear on your Web page. You can't actually see the applet running until you preview the exported site. The marker's dimensions probably won't correspond exactly to those of the applet when it's running, so plan your page layout accordingly. Also, bear in mind that a Java applet's user interface may look slightly different on each browser that displays it, even on the same operating system. The more preview tests you can run, for example using both Netscape Navigator and Microsoft Internet Explorer, the better.

To add a Java applet to a page:

1. Choose **Web Object...** from the Insert menu and select **Java Applet...** from the submenu.

2. In the dialog, click **Browse...** to locate the Applet Class File.

3. Click the upper **Add..** button to locate any other files required by the applet. You can hold down the **Ctrl** or **Shift** key to select multiple files in the dialog. To delete a file once you've added it to your list, click the file name and then click the **Delete** button.

4. If you do **not** wish to embed the files in your publication, uncheck the "Embed" option.

5. Click the lower **Add...** button to enter any required parameters (see documentation supplied with the Java applet). Add parameters one at a time, typing the Name and Value (excluding quotation marks) in the fields provided. To delete a parameter from the list (for example if you typed it wrong), click the **Up** or **Down** buttons to select the parameter, then click the **Delete** button below the list.

   When you publish your site, PagePlus will export and copy both embedded and non-embedded files into a common folder along with the HTML pages and graphics. Keep this in mind when entering file paths. If the applet's documentation insists on certain components being placed into separate subdirectories, you'll need to place them there "by hand" using an FTP utility.

6. Click **OK** to close the dialog, then click (or click and drag) with the cursor to place the Java marker on your page.

Adding HTML

While PagePlus's Web Publishing mode is not intended to support full-fledged HTML editing, it does allow you to add extra **HTML code** to a page. Using this approach, you can include HTML fragments generated by another application, copied from another Web page, or perhaps those you've written yourself.

PagePlus inserts a marker into your publication at the site where the HTML code will run. Since you won't be able to see the effect of the HTML until you preview the exported site, be careful to place the marker correctly. You'll definitely want to check your Web page in a browser! If there's a problem, double-check the code you entered and its position on the PagePlus page. If you have some grasp of HTML, examine the page source in a text editor such as Notepad or use your browser's "View Source" mode.

To add HTML code to a page:

1. Choose **Web Object...** from the Insert menu and select **HTML...** from the submenu.

2. The dialog includes one scrolling field for Body code, another for Header code. Enter one or more HTML code fragments into the appropriate field. To indent lines, press **Ctrl+Tab** to insert a tab. You can also use **Ctrl+C** to copy, **Ctrl+X** to cut, and **Ctrl+V** to paste via the Clipboard.

3. If the code calls for external files, use the **Add** button to locate them. Uncheck **Embed files in publication** if you want to keep the file(s) separate from your publication file.

4. Click **OK** to close the dialog, then click (or click and drag) with the cursor to place the HTML marker on your page.

Adding search engine descriptors

Although they're optional, if you want to increase the likelihood that your Web site will be "noticed" by major Web search services, you should enter **search engine descriptors (File>Web Site Properties>Search tab)**. Search services maintain catalogs of Web pages, often compiled through the use of "crawlers" or other programs that prowl the Web collecting data on sites and their content. By including descriptive information and keywords, you'll assist these engines in properly categorising your site.

Publishing a Web site to a local folder

Even though you may have saved your Web site as a PagePlus publication, it's not truly a "Web site" until you've converted it to HTML files and image files in a form that can be viewed in a Web browser. In PagePlus, this conversion process is called publishing the site. You can publish the site either to a local folder (on a hard disk) or to the World Wide Web itself. To review the basics, see **Getting started in Web mode** on p. 219.

Publishing the site to a local folder lets you preview the pages in your own browser prior to publishing them on the Web. You may find it convenient to keep your browser program open, and go back and forth between PagePlus and the browser. This way you can make changes to a single page in PagePlus, publish just the one page, then switch to your browser and preview that page to make sure everything appears just as you want it.

To publish the site to a local folder:

1. Choose **Web Site Properties...** from the File menu and double-check export settings, particularly those on the Graphics tab.

2. Choose **Publish Site** from the File menu and select **to Disk Folder...** from the submenu.

3. In the Publish to Disk Folder dialog, Choose the folder where you wish to store the output files, and if necessary, click **Make New Folder** to create a new folder.

4. To publish only one page (or a range of pages), check the page(s) to publish. This can save a lot of time by skipping the export of pages you haven't changed.

Previewing your Web site in a browser

Previewing your site in a Web browser is an essential step before publishing it to the World Wide Web. It's the only way you can see just how your PagePlus publication will appear to a visitor. Bear in mind that pages generally load much more quickly from a hard disk than they will over the Web. If performance is sluggish from a hard disk, it's time to subtract some graphics, divide the content into more (and smaller) pages, or run the Layout Checker again.

To preview your Web site from a local hard disk:

- Choose **Publish Site** from the File menu and select **to Disk Folder...** from the submenu. After publishing the site (or selected pages), answer **Yes** when asked if you want to run a Web browser to preview your pages.

  OR

- Choose **Preview Web Site in Browser...** from the File menu. Use the dialog to specify the page range by checking/unchecking pages. Click **OK** and the publication is exported to a temporary folder.

  OR

- (if you've previously published the site to a folder) Open your Web browser and use its Open File command to display a page from the site, usually the INDEX.HTML (Home Page) file.

Publishing to the World Wide Web

Publishing to the World Wide Web involves a few more steps, but is basically as simple as publishing to a local folder!

To publish your site to the World Wide Web:

1. Choose **Web Site Properties...** from the File menu and double-check export settings, particularly those on the Graphics tab.

2. Choose **Publish to Web...** from the File menu and select **to Web...** from the submenu.

3. If this is your first time publishing to the Web, the **Account Details** dialog will appear; otherwise you'll see **Publish to Web**. You'll need to set up at least one account before you can proceed.

4. In the Account Details dialog, enter the information you've gathered (see below):

   - The **Account name** can be any name of your choice. You'll use it to identify this account in PagePlus (in case you have more than one).

   - The **FTP address** of your Web host will be a specific URL starting with "ftp://" as supplied by your service provider.

   - Unless directed by your provider, you can leave the **Port number** set at "21."

- Leave the **Folder** box blank unless directed by your provider, or if you want to publish to a specific subfolder of your root directory.

- You'll also need a **Username** and **Password** as pre-assigned by the provider. Most likely these will correspond to e-mail login settings. Be sure to enter the password exactly as given to you, using correct upper- and lower-case spelling, or the host server may not recognise it. Check **Save password** to record the password on your computer, if you don't want to be bothered re-entering it with each upload.

- Click **OK** to close Account Details.

5. Once you've set up at least one account, the **Publish to Web** dialog appears. This lets you manage multiple accounts and give the go-ahead to publish files:

    - Select the account you want to use (if you've more than one). You can also use the dialog at this point to **Add** another account, **Edit** a selected account (for example, enter a new username or folder location), or **Delete** an account.

    - Make sure your Username and Password are correct, then click **Upload**.

    PagePlus seeks an Internet connection, then transfers your Web files to the host server you've designated. Only pages that have been updated since the last "publish" are transferred; any files with duplicate names are overwritten. You'll see a message when all files have been successfully copied.

6. You'll be able to see your page(s) "live" on the Web immediately. Point your Web browser to the URL including the path to the host server **plus** the folder to which you published.

Gathering server information

If you have an e-mail account, your contract with the e-mail service provider may allow you a certain amount of file space on their server where you can store files, including the files that comprise a Web site. Or you may have a separate "Web space" arrangement with a specialized Internet service provider. It's up to you to establish an account you can use for Web publishing.

Maintaining your Web site

Once you've **published your site** to the World Wide Web, you'll need to maintain the pages on your site by updating content periodically: adding or changing text, pictures, and links. Making the content changes is easy enough—all the originals are right there in your publication!

To maintain files and folders on your Web site:

1. Choose **Publish Site** from the File menu and select **Maintain Web Site...** from the submenu. The Account Details dialog appears.

2. Enter the address of the Web server, and your Username and Password. Type the correct path in the Folder box, if required by your provider. (For full details, see **Publishing to the World Wide Web** on p. 231.)

3. Click **OK**. PagePlus seeks an Internet connection and displays the designated folder's contents in the Maintain Web Site window.

4. Use standard Windows Explorer conventions to perform maintenance tasks:
   - Click on the column headers to change the current sort, or drag to change the column width.
   - The top row of buttons lets you view up one level, create a new folder, delete a selected item, or choose the view setting (Large Icons, Small Icons, List, or Details).
   - To rename a file or folder, click its name twice and then type, or right-click it and choose **Rename**.
   - You can **Ctrl**-click to select multiple files or **Shift**-click to select a range of files. Click the top-row **Delete** button or right-click an item and choose **Delete**.
   - To move one or more selected files, drag them into the destination folder.

When you're done, click the window's ⊠ **Close** button to terminate the FTP connection and return to PagePlus.

Index

Index

3D, 149
   filter effects, 149
   Instant 3D, 156

A

adjustments
   applying image, 133
Adobe Acrobat (PDF files), 193, 195
alignment, 88
animation effects
   adding to Web page, 226
artistic text, 78
   on a path, 79
Artistic Text tool, 79, 80
AutoCorrect, 102
   options, 47
AutoFit, 93
AutoFlow, 94
automatic text-fitting, 93
AutoRun, 12
AutoSpell, 102

B

banners
   printing, 187
Bevel effect, 148
Bézier curves, 140
Bitmap fills, 164
   adding to gallery, 168
bitmaps, 131
   importing (see also images), 131
bleed area guides, 39
blend modes, 152
BMP images, 131
booklets
   printing, 187
Bookmark Manager, 195
bookmarks
   for PDF files, 195
BookPlus, 118
books
   producing, 118
borders
   adding, 157
bullets and numbering, 88
   creating a list, 96
Bump Map effects, 150

C

Calendar Wizard, 114
Cap setting (lines), 144
character styles, 90
Character tab, 92
Characters
   special, 98
Clipboard, 53
   copying and pasting to or from, 53
closing PagePlus, 19
colour
   applying fill, 163, 164
   CMYK, 179
   creating your own, 172
   in PDF output, 193
   in Web publications, 224
   matching, 179
   output, 180
   palettes, 163, 172
   PANTONE, 179
   RGB, 179
   schemes, 169, 224
   screen, 180
   using, 163
Colour Fill, 149
Colour Management, 180
Colour Picker, 172
Colour Selector, 174
Colour tab, 163
column and row guides, 39
Combine Curves, 66
Comma button (tables), 113
Conical fills, 164
Conical transparency, 176
Context bar, 22
   Curve, 140, 143
   Curve Creation, 140
   Frame, 76
   Picture, 133
   Text, 88
correction lists, 101
Crop object to wrap outline, 66
Crop tools, 64

cropping objects, 64
Currency button (tables), 113
Curve context bar, 140, 143
Curve Creation context bar, 140
Curved Line tool, 139
curves (see lines), 139
Custom Format button (tables), 113
custom publication setup, 25
customising toolbars and tabs, 19

D

databases, 115
    importing, 115
date and time fields
    inserting, 98
Decimal buttons (tables), 113
Default paragraph font, 90
default properties, 46, 89
deforming objects (Mesh Warp), 67
design templates, 16, 99
device profiles, 180
dictionary, 104
    options, 47
    personal (spell-checking), 104
digital signatures, 213
dimensionality (Instant 3D), 156
dimensions, 25
    setting for publication, 25
document information, 100
    viewing, changing, and inserting, 100
dot grid, 43, 60
    snapping objects to, 44
draw-type images
    importing, 131
Drop Shadow effect, 148

E

edges
    adding, 157
editing text, 83, 86
effects
    filter, 148
    special (filter), 149
Ellipse fills, 164
E-mail
    hyperlinking to an address, 220
Emboss effect, 148

endnotes, 88
envelope, 67
    mesh warp, 67
exporting objects as image files, 62
exporting PDF files, 193

F

feathering (filter effect), 155
Feature list, 4
field labelling, 205
fill and line properties, 143, 164
Fill tool, 164
fills, 164
    adding Bitmap
        to gallery, 168
    adding gradient
        to gallery, 168
    Bitmap, 164
    changing colour or shading of, 163
    editing path of, 166
    gradient, 164
    using, 163
filter effects, 148, 149
Find & Replace, 87
Fit Text to Curve, 81
flipping objects, 64
folded publications, 187
    printing, 187
fonts
    listing in publication, 125
    setting, 88
    substituting, 125
footers, 44
footnotes, 88
    inserting, 88
Form Submit Wizard, 201, 208
Form toolbar, 201
formatting numbers in tables, 113
formulas (tables), 114
Frame context bar, 76
frame effect (border), 157
frame margins, 75
frame text, 72
frames
    applying fill colours to, 163, 164
    applying transparency, 175
    creating, 73
    for pictures, 131

layout of, 75
linking, 77
setup of, 75
Freehand Line tool, 139
functions (tables), 114

G

Gallery tab, 136
Getting started, 15
GIF animations
    adding to Web page, 226
GIF images
    used for Web, 225
Glow effect, 148
gradient colour fills, 164
    adding to gallery, 168
gradient transparency, 175
grammar
    checking with automatic proofreading, 105
grid
    spacing for dot, 43
groups, 53
    creating, 53
    resizing, 58
    ungrouping, 53
guides, 39
    for page margins, rows, columns, and bleeds, 39
    ruler, 42
    snapping objects to, 44

H

headers, 44
hotspots
    adding to Web page, 221
    editing, 222
Hyperlink Manager, 221
hyperlinks
    adding to Web page, 220
    in PDF files, 193
    setting colour of, 224
    viewing, 221
hyphenation, 100

I

ICC, 180
images, 131
    adjusting, 133
    borders for, 157
    colourising, 163
    converting objects to, 61
    default sizes, 57
    embedding vs. linking, 133
    exporting objects as, 62
    for Web (overview), 225
    importing, 131
    listing imported images in publication, 124
    resizing, 57
    setting default properties, 46
    setting size when pasting, 53
    setting transparency of bitmaps, 175
    sizing imported or pasted, 59
    wrapping text around, 95
importing
    database tables, 115
    images, 131
    paint- and draw-type images, 131
    styles, 92
    text, 71
imposition
    of folded publications, 187
indents
    setting, 84
index
    creating, 117
Installation, 11
Instant 3D, 156
interface
    customising toolbars and tabs, 19
    view options, 28

J

Java applets
    adding to Web page, 227
Javascript
    validating forms with, 206
Join setting (lines), 144
JPEG images
    used for Web, 225

K

kerning, 88
   adjusting, 92

L

layers
   adding, 33
   and master pages, 35
   rearranging, 34
   removing, 33
   selecting objects on, 34
   viewing, 30
   working with, 32
layout
   options, 47
layout guides, 44
   setting, 40
layout tools, 39, 41, 44
   rulers, 41
   snapping, 44
letterspacing (tracking), 92
   adjusting, 92
lighting, 149
   3D Effect, 149
line and fill properties, 143, 164
Linear fills, 164
linear transparency, 175, 176
lines
   calligraphic, 144
   changing colour or shading of, 163
   closing (to make shapes), 146
   combining, 66
   dashed, 144
   drawing, 139
   editing, 142
   fitting text to, 79
   resizing, 57
   setting properties of, 143
linking
   text frames, 77
locking object size or position, 59

M

mail and photo merge, 123

margins, 39
   mirrored, 40
   setting, 39
marquees
   animated
      adding to Web page, 226
master pages
   adding, 31
   adding and removing, 31
   and layers, 35
   deleting, 32
   headers and footers on, 44
   overview, 27
   page numbers on, 45
   rearranging, 31
   removing, 31
   viewing and editing, 30
Master pages, 26
measuring objects, 41
Mesh Warp toolbar, 67
metafiles
   importing, 131
mirrored margins, 40
Multipage view, 29
multiple documents, 17
multiple pages, 106
   print preview, 106, 186
   printing, 188
   viewing, 29
multiple selections, 52

N

named styles, 91
navigation, 30
Normal style, 90
Normal view, 29

O

object styles, 158
objects
   aligning, 60
   applying mesh warp, 67
   arranging, 59
   converting to pictures, 61
   copying, 53
   cropping, 64
   distributing, 60

duplicating, 54
flipping, 64
locking size or position, 59
measuring, 41
moving, 55
ordering, 32
pasting, 54
pasting formatting of, 55
replicating, 54
resizing, 57
reusing in different publications, 136
rotating, 63
selecting, 51
selecting more than one, 52
setting default properties, 46
snapping to dot grid or guides, 44
Opacity tab, 176
opening an existing publication, 17
options
   setting, 47
oval
   drawing, 145

P

Page Manager, 30, 31
page margin guides, 39
Page Setup, 25
page size and orientation, 25
   setting, 25
pages
   adding, 31
   numbering, 45
   rearranging, 31
   removing, 31
   turning, 30
   viewing, 28
Pages tab, 30, 31
paint-type images, 131
   importing, 131
Palette Manager, 174
palettes
   themed, 172
palettes
   colour, 172
   publication, 163
   standard, 163
PANTONE, 179
paragraph styles, 90

paragraphs, 88
pasteboard area, 28
Path flyout, 80
path text, 79
Pattern Map effects, 150
PDF
   adding bookmarks to, 195
   exporting, 193
   importing, 193
   publishing, 189, 193
PDF forms
   collecting data from, 207
   creating, 201
   designing, 198
   field labelling for, 205
   form field properties in, 205
   importing data into, 211
   using, 196
   validating, 206
PDF/X, 189
Percent button (tables), 113
photographs, 131
   importing, 131
PhotoPlus
   editing images with, 134
   editing SPP files with, 134
Picture context bar, 133
pictures
   converting objects to, 61
   deforming (Mesh Warp), 67
   importing (see also images), 131
PNG images, 226
polygon
   drawing, 145
posters
   printing, 187
PostScript output, 189
previewing the printed page, 106, 186
previewing Web sites in Web browser, 230
printing, 185
   basics and options, 185
   of banners, posters, and booklets, 187
   PDF files, 193
   previewing the page, 106, 186
   professional, 189
   saving print profiles, 190
profiles (device), 180

proofing tools
    previewing the printed page, 106, 186
    Proof Reader, 105
    Resource Manager, 124
    Spell Checker, 104
    Thesaurus, 105
Publication palette, 163, 172
    adding custom colours to. *See*
    adding PANTONE colours to, 174
publications
    creating with design templates, 16
    for World Wide Web, 219
    layers, 26
    master pages, 27
    opening existing, 17
    producing books, 118
    saving, 18
    setting dimensions, 25
    starting from scratch, 16
    working with multiple, 17
publishing Web sites
    to local folder, 230
    to World Wide Web, 231

Q

QuickClear and QuickFill (tables), 111
QuickShape tool, 145

R

Radial fills, 164
Radial transparency, 176
raster effect options, 47
raster images, 131
    importing, 131
readability
    checking with Proof Reader, 105
registration, 11
replication
    of objects, 54
Resource Manager, 124
resources
    listing imported resources in
        publication, 124
reverting to saved version, 17
RGB, 179
rollover buttons
    adding to Web page, 222

Rotate tool, 63
row and column guides, 39
ruled lines
    creating, 97
ruler guides, 42
rulers
    adjusting, 41
    options, 47

S

saving a publication, 18
scaling
    printing effect, 187
Scheme Manager, 224
schemes, 224
    colour, 169, 224
Schemes tab, 169
SDB (Serif Database) files, 124
search engines
    adding descriptors to Web site, 229
selecting objects, 51
Serif Colour Chart, 179, 181
Serif PhotoPlus (SPP) files, 134
Serif Web Resources, 208
service provider (server) information,
    232
SFM (Serif Font Map) files, 126
Shade/Tint slider, 165
Shadow effect, 148
Shaped Frame tool, 74
shapes
    applying transparency, 175
    changing fill colours, 163
    closing, 146
    combining, 66
    drawing and editing, 145
    fitting text to, 79
    resizing, 57
signatures, 213
    digital, 213
snapping, 44
sound
    adding to Web page, 227
special effects, 148, 149
Spell Checker, 103, 104
spelling aids, 102, 103
stacking order, 32
standalone text, 78

Standard Frame tool, 74
stars
   drawing, 145
starting PagePlus, 15
Startup Wizard, 15, 16
   turning off, 17
story editor (WritePlus), 86
story text, 72
   flowing in frame sequence, 76
Straight Line tool, 139
Studio tabs
   customising, 21
style (of font), 88
Style Attributes Editor, 53, 159
styles
   importing, 92
   object, 158
   text (see also text styles), 89
substitution
   of fonts, 125
support, technical, 11
Swatches tab, 143, 148, 163, 164
System requirements, 11

T

tab stops, 85
table of contents
   creating, 116
Table tool, 108
tables, 114
   autoformat of, 110
   calendars, 114
   creating, 108
   formatting numbers, 113
   inserting formulas, 114
   manipulating, 108
   overview, 107
   QuickClear and QuickFill, 111
tabs
   switching off all Studio, 21
   customising Studio, 21
   resetting layout of Studio, 22
   saving layout of Studio, 22
technical support, 11
template (*.PPX) files, 18
text
   adding to text frame, 74
   artistic (standalone), 78

AutoCorrect and AutoSpell, 101
   changing colour or shading of, 163
   creating ruled lines, 97
   editing on the page, 83
   editing with WritePlus, 86
   Find & Replace, 87
   fitting to frames, 93
   formatting in PagePlus, 88
   importing from file, 71, 89
   inserting date/time, 99
   inserting user details, 99
   kerning, 92
   letterspacing, 92
   on a path, 79
   on a path, editing, 81
   setting default properties, 46, 89
   special effects, 149
   special effects for, 148
   styles, 89
   tables (overview), 107
   Unicode, 85, 98
   using gradient and Bitmap fills, 78, 164
   wrap, 94
Text context bar, 88
text frames, 72
   setting default properties of, 46
Thesaurus, 105
thumbnails
   printing, 188
tiling
   in printing, 188
time field
   inserting, 99
tool
   Artistic Text, 79
   Crop, 64
   Curved Line, 139
   Freehand Line, 139
   QuickShape, 145
   Rotate, 63
   Shaped Frame, 74
   Standard Frame, 74
   Straight Line, 139
   Table, 108
   Transparency, 176

toolbar
    Attributes, 68, 156, 166, 177
    Form, 201
    Mesh Warp, 67
    options, 47
    Tools, 157
    View, 28
toolbars
    customising, 19
Tooltips
    set options for, 47
Transform tab, 56, 58
transparency, 175
Transparency tool, 176
tutorials, 12
typeface
    setting, 88

U

Unicode text, 85, 98
user details
    inserting, 99

V

validation
    of PDF forms, 206
vector images, 131
    importing, 131
video
    adding to Web page, 227
view options, 28

W

warping objects, 67
Web colours, 224
Web Publishing mode, 219

Web sites
    adding animation effects, 226
    adding HTML code, 229
    adding Java applets, 227
    adding rollover buttons, 222
    adding search engine descriptors, 229
    adding sound and video, 227
    choosing Web site colours, 224
    getting started, 219
    image settings (overview), 225
    maintaining, 233
    previewing in Web browser, 230
    publishing to local folder, 230
    publishing to World Wide Web, 231
    setting page and file properties, 226
    viewing hyperlinks in publication, 221
    working with hotspots, 221
web-ready PDF forms, 208
What's New, 4
Wizards
    set options for, 47
WMF images, 131
word processor files, 71
workspace
    customising toolbars and tabs, 19
    resetting layout of, 22
    saving, 22
World Wide Web, 219
wrap outline, 66
    using to crop object, 66
wrapping text around objects, 94
WritePlus, 86, 117

Z

zero point, 41
zoom view options, 29

Notes

The remaining pages are provided for you to make your own notes.